STRINGS
backstage

21st - Century

String Quartets

Volume 1

Edith Eisler

STRING LETTER PUBLISHING

Publisher: David A. Lusterman
Editorial Director: Jeffrey Pepper Rodgers
Editor: Mary VanClay
Associate Editor: Jessamyn Reeves-Brown
Assistant Editor: Marsha Gonick
Designer: Ann Leonardi
Production Coordinator: Christi Payne
Marketing Manager: Jennifer Fujimoto

Front cover: Emerson String Quartet, photo by Christian Steiner.
Back cover: Guarneri String Quartet, photo by Philips Classics Productions; Tokyo String Quartet, photo by Christian Steiner; Orion String Quartet, photo by Nora Feller.

Printed in the United States of America.
All rights reserved.
This book was produced by String Letter Publishing, Inc.
PO Box 767
San Anselmo, California 94979
(415) 485-6946
www.stringsmagazine.com

Library of Congress Cataloging-in-Publication Data

Eisler, Edith.
    21st-century string quartets / by Edith Eisler.
        p.   cm. -- (Strings backstage)
        Contents: v. 1. American String Quartet. Borodin String Quartet. Emerson String Quartet. Guarneri String Quartet. Juilliard String Quartet. Mandelring String Quartet. Manhattan String Quartet. Mendelssohn String Quartet. Orion String Quartet. St. Petersburg String Quartet. Tokyo String Quartet.
        ISBN 1-890490-15-6
        1. String quartets (Musical groups) I. Title: Twenty-first-century string quartets. II. Title. III. Series.

ML 398 .E37 2000
785'.7194—dc21

                                                                        99-054129

STRING LETTER PUBLISHING

TABLE OF CONTENTS

INTRODUCTION

The music that has been written for string quartet is some of the most beloved in all of classical-music literature. For many, the string quartet epitomizes chamber-music performance, and the very name *chamber music* points up the intimacy that was once the norm for both performer and audience. Although today most concerts are held in auditoriums rather than private salons, nevertheless the music itself, and the personal involvement of the four players, still casts a spell over listeners and their emotions.

Like the music itself, however, life as a string-quartet member is complex. As Joel Smirnoff of the Juilliard String Quartet (page 28) explains, "the art of chamber-music playing is the art of being able to produce something beautiful while you are listening very carefully to what's going on around you, and adapting to it and making changes on the spur of the moment, in time and pitch, and in terms of both technical and interpretive things." Each musical part is essential and must be heard, yet all the voices must blend into a whole that speaks with a different voice than any of the individual parts.

And the challenge is not simply technical. While the soloist, as star of the show, may have to deal with loneliness as well as acclaim, the quartet player must constantly communicate, negotiate, compromise, and share with other equally dedicated, talented, and opinionated musicians. Players who create and maintain the personal and musical relationships necessary in a fine quartet have achieved a special kind of magic.

The 11 quartets profiled in this book represent some of the most talented chamber musicians of our time. They are passionate in their discussions of the most famous—and at times the most problematic—works in the genre: the quartets of Beethoven, Shostakovich, Janáček, Bartók, Schoenberg, and others. Their explanations of how they work through the music, from the practice room to the stage, can inform and inspire. Just as the music speaks to us all, so do the musicians, since their basic lessons pertain not only to quartet players but also to humans in any relationship: learn to speak up—diplomatically—and learn to listen.

Mary VanClay
Editor

The Emerson String Quartet

The Emerson String Quartet is a prizewinning ensemble with an appetite for big projects. Recording exclusively on Deutsche Grammophon, the group has won four Grammy Awards (for best classical album and best chamber-music performance). The players have spent nearly two decades as faculty members at the Hartt School of Music of the University of Hartford in Connecticut, where they run a special training program for young quartets. Each of the musicians maintains an active solo schedule, and cellist David Finckel, with his wife, pianist Wu Han, also codirects the SummerFest La Jolla series and cofounded a recording company called ArtistLed.

In the 1980s, the Emerson Quartet gained national attention for presenting the six Bartók quartets in a single evening—first at Alice Tully Hall, and later at its debut at Carnegie Hall. In this 1997 interview, the group discusses its then-current project of performing and recording the complete Beethoven quartets. Now, in 1999–2000, it is performing the complete Shostakovich quartets and has just released a new CD set of the works, having recorded them live at Aspen.

Beethoven to Bartók

"I still remember the first tour I did with [the group]," says Lawrence Dutton, violist of the Emerson String Quartet. "We started in Corpus Christi, Texas, went on to Oak Ridge, Tennessee, Mobile, Alabama—all little places. And after expenses, I think we each made $50, and if my mother hadn't picked me up at the airport, I'd only have made $25."

"In 1979, that wasn't so bad," comments violinist Philip Setzer. "At least we came out ahead."

Since then, the Emerson Quartet, whose other members are violinist Eugene Drucker and cellist David Finckel, has become one of the most sought-after groups of its kind, with an extensive discography on Deutsche Grammophon to its credit and more than 100 concerts a year in the world's most prestigious concert halls. This keeps the players so relentlessly busy that I have to catch them during breaks in rehearsals and recording sessions, and separately over the telephone. Yet they seem entirely unruffled: concentrating on the matter at hand, they talk about their highly unusual programming with zest and enthusiasm, about the music they play with thoughtful eloquence, about the present state of classical music with passionate concern. Yet always lurking around the corner in even the most serious discussion is the witty riposte, the humorous twinkle of the eye.

Of the four Emerson players, Dutton is the only one who does not come from a family of musicians. Setzer's parents were both violinists in the Cleveland Orchestra under George Szell. Drucker's father, Ernest, was a violinist in the Metropolitan Opera Orchestra and had been a member of the famous Busch Quartet as well as of the Busch chamber orchestra. I met him when I joined that group—my very first job in America—so talking about him stirred up many cherished memories. "My father told me he knew you," Drucker notes. "And do you know [violinist] Adolf Busch's collected letters, called *Letters, Pictures, Memories* (Arts and Letters Press [PO Box 101, Walpole, NH 03608-0101], 1991)? It was to my father that he wrote his last letter, congratulating him on the birth of a second son—me."

Finckel's father is the composer Edwin Finckel, whose entire works for cello the younger Finckel has recorded with his wife and regular partner, pianist Wu Han. The family is full of cellists. "At present, the two most active are Chris, who plays in the Manhattan Quartet, and Michael; they are my cousins," Finckel says. "Their father, George, taught at Bennington College for years and was a member of many distinguished groups. But I also have grandfathers who were cellists, and my great-uncle Alden was principal cellist of the National Symphony under Hans Kindler."

Asked about the background of the current Emerson String Quartet, Finckel says, "The background is so far back, I don't even remember it."

"Especially because you weren't there at the beginning," Drucker retorts. He continues, "Philip and I started playing together as students at the Juilliard School in the 1970s, long before the official existence of the quartet. We had various violists and cellists and probably played two or three concerts a year while we slowly learned the repertoire. Then in the 1976–77 season, we decided to try to make a professional career as a quartet. Since it was the bicentennial year of the United States, we wanted to name it after an American with cultural associations, and we chose Ralph Waldo Emerson. We did our first tour and a recording for New World Records in the spring of 1977; Larry came into the quartet in June. That summer, we had our first residency at the

Vermont Mozart Festival. The next season, we had 20 concerts, which seemed a lot to us, and in 1978, we won the [Walter W.] Naumburg [International Competition], which sponsored our New York debut in 1979. And that fall, David joined us. Phil had had a trio with him and knew his playing, so he came highly recommended."

"I still had to take a grueling audition," Finckel mutters.

"It was very impressive," says Drucker, "because we made you play everything from a Mozart cello quartet to Webern and Bartók."

Dutton interrupts, "When I auditioned, I was only 23 and still had a year left at Juilliard."

"You were also very impressive," Drucker assures him. "We chose you from among 11 violists, while we auditioned only two cellists."

Dutton grins. "That's a viola joke: you need 11 violists to find *one*."

There is also a violin joke about the lady who comes backstage after a string-quartet concert and asks the second violinist to show her his instrument. "You see," she explains, "I've always wanted to know what a second violin looks like!" The Emerson Quartet's violinists have their own answer: they alternate, and what strikes the listener is that although Drucker and Setzer are entirely different in tone, style, and approach and each can put the stamp of his own personality on the music, each can also melt homogeneously into the whole. Though the alternating lightens the burden of leadership, doesn't it make programming more complicated? "Sometimes it does," Setzer admits. "Originally, we tried to switch at intermission, but we couldn't keep that up. Now we just try to avoid having one person lead a whole program."

Werner Neumeister

From left: David Finckel, Lawrence Dutton, Eugene Drucker, and Philip Setzer.

Choosing who was to play which part was, according to Setzer, very simple. "At one point early on, we sat down with the whole repertoire and divided everything right down the middle; there's no expert in any style. If one of us feels strongly about playing first violin in a particular piece, fine, he'll do it; otherwise, we let it depend on how the programs shape up. It's not a big deal."

This leads to a discussion of their programs, which have always been extraordinarily imaginative. "Phil is the architect of our programming, and he's very good at it," says Drucker, "though of course the rest of us have to approve his suggestions."

It was Setzer's idea to present complete quartet cycles in chronological order, so as to follow the composer's creative development and experience in writing the works. The first time the Emerson used this approach was in 1981 at New York's Alice Tully Hall, for a performance of the six Bartók quartets—all in a single evening. The reason, Finckel explains, was that "if you split them between two programs, one

What they play

Both violinists use the same strings: Dominant G, D, and A, and Corelli E. Setzer plays a Nicolas Lupot violin made in Orléans in 1793 and an Albert Nürnberger bow. Drucker's violin is an Antonio Stradivari made in Cremona in 1686, his bow an early Pajeot, and his spare bow a Millant. He remarks, "When people come backstage and say, 'Oh, what a wonderful violin!' I always wonder whether the program mentioned that it's a Strad. If it did, I don't give much value to such comments, because people expect a Strad to sound great. But if they don't know what it is, then it makes me feel very happy."

Dutton plays a Pietro Giovanni Mantegazza viola made in Milan in 1796, and a ca. 1920 Eugene Sartory and a ca.-1850 Pierre Simon bow— "at the same time," he jokes. (The Simon is his primary bow.) He decided Dominant strings were not strong enough ("for the two bows," interject the others) and switched to Helicore by D'Addario.

Finckel has many bows, but these days he most often uses a modern one made by Bernard Walke in Ottawa, Canada (although at the time of this interview he favored a Sartory). He uses Thomastik strings exclusively, a combination of Spirocores and Bel Cantos. His instrument collection is the most unusual, and he talks about it with enormous enthusiasm. "I have two cellos," he says, "one by Giovanni Battista Guadagnini, made in 1754 in Milan, and one by Samuel Zygmuntowicz, made in 1993 in Brooklyn."

Finckel commissioned the latter instrument from Zygmuntowicz after hearing one of the maker's violins that Drucker had just purchased. "I just fell in love with its sound—it spoke to me; I felt I had a special affinity for that tone quality," Finckel explains. "So I decided I wanted to see if this man would make a cello for me. We met and talked about models and which cellos he would like to copy. I knew I could gain access to one of them, the famous 'Duport' Stradivari, which belongs to Rostropovich, who is a very good friend of mine. I showed him Gene's violin and he was so impressed that, though he doesn't usually allow anyone to copy his cello, he made an exception for Sam."

The instrument was completed after five years of careful work, and Finckel loved it from the start. He adds, "Of course, my Guadagnini is a wonderful cello and I still play it, but I'm a great believer in the young makers of today; they're making better instruments than ever before, and, based on my own experience, I think they are going to save us, as old instruments are increasingly being priced out of the range of performers. One of the most wonderful, rewarding moments I can have as a cellist is to take an instrument from a young maker and see the expression on his face when I play on it and bring it to life."

becomes too short, the other too long. The only way to play them chronologically is in one concert." The resulting marathon of three hours and 40 minutes created a sensation. Finckel recalls that concert with a chuckle, saying, "I had only been with the quartet a couple of years, and it nearly killed me. By now, of course, we've done it so many times that it's no longer so difficult."

The group repeated the program at Carnegie Hall in 1988 and at Avery Fisher Hall in 1995 as part of the Bartók commemoration, and has taken it all over the world. "Actually, most operas are longer," Drucker points out, "but still, it's quite a lot for the listener, so the real test is to have just as many people there at the end as at the beginning." Having heard both the Alice Tully and Avery Fisher Hall marathons, I can testify that the audience not only became no smaller but seemed increasingly spellbound by the cumulative impact of the music.

The Bartók quartets also occupy a special place in the Emerson's discography: the recording won two Grammys and two major European awards and has become a classic. It was always a bestseller, a fact the players talk about with modesty as well as down-to-earth realism. After admitting that the awards attracted attention, Dutton says, "I guess we were lucky. At the time we released the recording, there was little competition on compact disc. The old recordings of the great Juilliard or Hungarian Quartets were on LP."

Drucker adds, "It was the first recording of the cycle on two CDs; most people do it on three. Also, it came out around the time we played our second marathon, which created a certain amount of momentum."

"And the fact that we played all over the world and had a strong presence on public radio also helped," Setzer notes. "We had a big reputation before we started making records."

This season, the Emerson is involved in presenting another, much bigger, cycle, one which, in Drucker's words, is "not only among the masterpieces of the literature, but among the monuments of Western culture"—that is, the Beethoven quartets. The players favor performing them, too, in chronological order.

"It works very well in six concerts," Dutton explains. "The first two are purely Op. 18. Then you have a big program of the three Op. 59s, which is really great because they are so symphonic. It's very effective in big halls; we did it at Avery Fisher. Next comes Op. 74, the 'Harp,' and Op. 95, which is not very long, and then Op. 127, the transition that leads to the late quartets. That's a pretty long program. Then you have Op. 132 and Op. 130 with the *Grosse Fuge,* and the last concert has Op. 131, Op. 135, and ends with the alternate finale of Op. 130. The cycle is fascinating in chronological order, especially if you have the same audience for the whole journey."

Setzer adds, "Yes, to be there from the beginning of Op. 18, No. 3, which was the first one he actually wrote, to the very end, is a really powerful experience."

"We've also played the quartets in a sort of modified chronological order, with two Op. 18s and one Op. 59 on each of the first three programs, then proceeding chronologically to the end," Dutton continues. "And of course we've played them in the way most people do them—one early, one middle, and one late quartet on each program."

But Setzer's inspired inventiveness has also found an infinite variety of combinations that "bounce the Beethoven quartets off those of other composers," as he puts it. "We've programmed the late Beethoven with the late Schubert quartets; that works very well not only because they are all great masterpieces, but because they were written at about the same time and at the end of both composers' lives. And we've combined the late quartets of Beethoven and Shostakovich, who share certain revolutionary tendencies. Beethoven was fighting against what was expected of him, pushing against the confines of the genre and of classical music in general to make them fit what he needed to say, and Shostakovich—well, everybody knows by now under what sort of restraints and constraints he was writing during the Soviet era, and that he expressed—and often encoded—in his music, especially his chamber music, all the thoughts and emotions he could not voice openly."

Christian Steiner

In 1997, the Emerson recorded the complete Beethoven quartets; next they turned to the complete quartets of Shostakovich.

The success of that coupling sparked the Emerson's latest project: an eight-concert series over two seasons at Alice Tully Hall, combining the complete Beethoven quartets with masterpieces of the 20th century. "Beethoven was so much ahead of his time that his music is a bridge not only to the 19th, but also the 20th century," Drucker says. "Stravinsky—who was not a great admirer of his—called the *Grosse Fuge* the first real 20th-century piece of music."

Setzer explains the programs in some detail. "The first year, we're concentrating on Beethoven's early and middle periods: three Op. 18s, starting with his first one, No. 3; and the three Op. 59s, Op. 74, and 95. And from the early part of the 20th century, we've chosen composers who are linked to Beethoven either by connection or antithesis: Ravel, who was influenced by Beethoven's technique of using and reworking small motivic kernels; Barber, whose Adagio is based on an earlier style with its quasi-medieval harmonies, recalling Beethoven's Op. 132; Janáček, whose "Kreutzer" Sonata, though inspired by Tolstoy's story, also obliquely refers to Beethoven's sonata. It even contains a musical quote from it, though it's so well-hidden that it took me years to find it: the step-wise progression that opens the third movement of the quartet recalls the chorale theme in the first movement of the sonata.

"Then there's Stravinsky and Bartók for contrast, and Webern, who was both romantic and intellectual and provided a bridge to the 20th century. And the first program includes Schoenberg's *Verklärte Nacht,* which is really pre–20th-century and is also a transitional work. Joining us for this are Eric Shumsky, the son of our teacher Oscar Shumsky, on viola, and Roberta Cooper, Gene Drucker's wife, on cello. The second year will cover the other three Op. 18s and all the late quartets of Beethoven, coupled with Ives, Berg's *Lyric Suite,* Shostakovich, and Wolfgang Rhim. Obviously, you can't deal with the whole 20th century in eight concerts; this is just an overview."

The quartet continued its Beethoven immersion on its latest record-ing, a seven-disc set of the complete cycle. Unusual in several respects, it is coming out not in the customary format of three consecutive vol-umes—early, middle, and late quartets—but all at once. And it is in chronological order—almost. "To be strictly chronological," Setzer explains, "it would have had to be stretched to eight CDs, two of them quite short, and we all decided against that, as long as some sense of chronology was preserved. So now, the early and middle quartets, in the order in which they were written, make up the first four CDs. Only the late ones are slightly out of sequence: Opp. 127 and 131 on disc 5, Opp. 132 and 135 on disc 6. The final disc has Op. 130 with the *Grosse Fuge,* then the alternate finale, with a long space in between, so it doesn't sound like the seventh movement of the quartet. In this way, if people want to listen to Op. 130 with the alternate finale, they can just skip the Fugue, though we're really trying to discourage that: we always play the piece with the Fugue and don't consider the other finale an appropriate ending to the whole quartet. On the other hand, it's the very last piece Beethoven wrote before he died, so it makes a good postscript."

Drucker adds, "I think it's interesting to have both finales on the same record, just to show what the second was supposed to substitute for."

The most unique feature of the recording, however, is an extra disc added to the complete set, on which the players talk about the music in general and then play several entire movements, preceding each with brief comments on the music's character and place in Beethoven's life. The disc is meant to be used on radio stations in conjunction with broadcasts of the music, and it should serve to make the quartets more easily acces-sible to listeners unfamiliar with them. I was allowed to eavesdrop on the last half-hour of the final taping and found it fascinating.

"We all know that the classical-music recording industry is facing grave problems," Drucker says in explanation of the "talking" CD. "When CDs first came out, they generated a great revival of interest in classical recordings, because everybody was replacing their LPs. But CDs don't have to be replaced; they don't become scratched or obsolete and they last forever. That puts the industry in a very difficult position. Besides, classical music generally, in our present culture, is going through a crisis. One reason is that public music education is being neglected; another is that nowadays people want the kind of 'entertain-

Recordings

American Contemporaries: *Harbison: String Quartet No. 2; Wernick: String Quartet No. 4; Schuller: String Quartet No. 3 (DG 437 537).*

American Originals: *Ives: String Quartet No. 1, "From the Salvation Army"; String Quartet No. 2; Scherzo, "Holding Your Own"; Barber: String Quartet Op. 11 (DG 435 864).*

Barber: The Complete Songs, Dover Beach; Harbison: String Quartet No. 2; Wernick: String Quartet No. 4; Schuller: String Quartet No. 3. With Thomas Hampson, baritone (DG 435 867).

Bartók: Complete String Quartets (DG 423 657).

Beethoven: Complete String Quartets (DG 447 076).

Beethoven: Quartet in F Minor, Op. 95; Schubert: Quartet No. 14 in D Minor, D. 810, "Death and the Maiden" (DG 423 398).

Beethoven: Quartet in F, Op. 135; Schubert: Quartet in G, D. 887 (DG 429 224).

Brahms: Quartet No. 1 in C Minor, Op. 51; Schumann: Quartet in A, Op. 41, No. 3 (DG 431 650).

Cacioppo: Monsterslayer. With Curt Cacioppo, piano (CPS 8652).

Cowell: Quartet Euphometric; Harris: Three Variations on a Theme (Quartet No. 2); Shepherd: Triptych for Soprano and String Quartet. With Betsy Norden, soprano (NW 218).

Debussy: Quartet in G Minor, Op. 10; Ravel: Quartet in F (DG 427 320).

Dvořák: Quartet in E-Flat, Op. 87; Quintet in A, Op. 81. With Menahem Pressler, piano. (DG 439 868).

Dvořák: Quartet No. 12 in F, Op. 96; Smetana: Quartet No. 1 in E Minor, "From My Life" (DG 429 723).

Dvořák: Quartet No. 12 in F, Op. 96, "American"; Smetana: Quartet No. 1 in E Minor, "From My Life"; Brahms: Quartet No. 1 in C Minor, Op. 51; Schumann: Quartet in A, Op. 41, No. 3; Borodin: Quartet No. 2 in D; Tchaikovsky: Quartet No. 1 in D, Op. 11; Debussy: Quartet in G Minor, Op. 10; Ravel: Quartet in F Major (Book of the Month Records 21-7526, four volumes).

Imbrie: Quartet No. 4; Schuller: Quartet No. 2 (NW 212).

Mozart: Flute Quartets Nos. 1–4. With Carol Wincenc, flute (DG 431 770).

Mozart: The "Haydn" Quartets (DG 431 797).

Mozart: Quartet in B-Flat, K. 458; Quartet in C, K. 465; Haydn: Quartet in C, Op. 76, No. 3 (DG 427 657).

Mozart: Quartet in G, K. 387; Quartet in D Minor, K. 421 (DG 439 861).

Piston: Concerto for String Quartet, Winds and Percussion. With the Juilliard Orchestra (S-248).

Prokofiev: Quartet No. 1 in B Minor, Op. 50; Sonata for Two Violins, Op. 56; Quartet No. 2 in F, Op. 92 (DG 431 772).

Rorem: Quartet No. 4; Edgar Meyer: String Quintet. With Edgar Meyer, double bass (DG 453 606).

Schubert: String Quintet; Late Quartets. With Mstislav Rostropovich, cello (DG 459 151).

Schubert: String Quintet. With Mistislav Rostropovich, cello (DG 431 792).

Schumann: Quintet for Piano, 2 Violins, Viola, and Cello in E-Flat, Op. 44; Quartet for Piano, Viola, and Cello in E-Flat, Op. 47. With Menahem Pressler, piano (DG 445 848).

Shostakovich: Quartet No. 8 (DG 459 670).

Shostakovich: Complete Quartets (DG 463 284).

Tchaikovsky: Quartet No. 1 in D, Op. 11; Borodin: Quartet No. 2 in D (DG 427 618).

Webern: Slow Movement for String Quartet; Five Movements for String Quartet, Op. 5; String Quartet (1905); Six Bagatelles for String Quartet, Op. 9; Rondo for String Quartet (1906); Movement for String Trio, Op. Post.; Three Pieces for String Quartet; String Trio, Op. 20; String Quartet, Op. 28 (DG 445 828).

ment' they get from television or computers—not just music, but verbal
and visual stimulation as well. And considering that the computer soft-
ware that offers all these extra elements only costs about the same as a
CD, it's not surprising that it has become more difficult to sell audio
recordings, which also lack the visual element of a live concert, where
people can see the musicians interacting and actually making music."

Would going to more concerts make people want to buy more
records? "It apparently doesn't work that way," Dutton answers. "It's true
that the so-called 'core' concert-going and the 'core' record-buying public overlap to some extent, but though it seems a reasonable expecta-
tion, no evidence has ever been found that you can increase the one by
increasing the other."

Setzer breaks in, "The other night on television, I had a good example of the kind of mentality classical music is up against. Torville and
Dean, the famous ice-skaters, were performing a dance for which Dean,
who is a very gifted choreographer and a great artist, had used a
Sarabande from one of Bach's cello suites, taped by Yo-Yo Ma. It was
very beautiful, but at the end the judges marked them down because
the music did not have a 'consistent beat.' Isn't that the ultimate irony—
no beat in a Baroque dance?"

Drucker agrees and adds, "When you bring out a big set like the
Beethoven quartets, you try to reach beyond the core audience, which
is actually very small. I think probably more people know about
Beethoven's symphonies, and about his historical role in the development of Western music, than about his quartets, because unfortunately
chamber music is still stigmatized in many people's minds as an elitist,
stuffy, stodgy art form. But when Beethoven was writing his music, it
was considered anything but stodgy, and that's what we're trying to get
across on the 'talking' CD. We also try to tell the people who are afraid
of not understanding the music that it isn't necessary to know how it's
put together; it's enough to sit back and surrender to the emotional
experience."

Finckel suggests, "It's like looking at a mountain range: you can
admire its grandeur without knowing what stone it's made of. So we
talked about the quartets and about the different periods, and then we
selected ten movements to focus on."

"It was difficult," Setzer interjects, "because we couldn't say too
much, but we didn't want to transfer Beethoven into the world of the
soundbite."

"Basically, we were looking for movements that we felt contained
some of Beethoven's most important writing, or had a special dimension, either of profundity or programmatic content," Drucker explains.
"For example, we chose the slow movement of Op. 18, No. 1, because
it's supposed to be based on the tomb scene in *Romeo and Juliet*, and the
first movement of Op. 18, No. 4, because it shows Beethoven's stormy
side. It's in the same key as the fifth symphony and the third piano con-

certo and, with its brooding and obsessive feeling, represents a real breakthrough in the early quartets. We also picked movements that had a story connected to them and lent themselves to being talked about, like the Cavatina from Op. 130. Beethoven is said to have been moved to tears while writing it and on his deathbed referred to it as his favorite work. It contains a passage with a half-sobbing, half-stammering melody that's marked *beklemmt*, which could be translated as 'choked,' though it has an emotional as well as a physical implication."

Setzer adds, "Let's say the pieces we talked about are no more important than the rest, but by choosing some that had a personal aspect, we hoped to bring the audience in closer contact with Beethoven himself. Of course many composers have used the string quartet as a vehicle for their deepest, most intimate feelings; there are passages in the Beethoven quartets that are so personal that I feel like an intruder trespassing on his privacy. I think if you approach the music in this way, almost like his journal, it will be less intimidating, because you can relate it to his life and his fate, especially in the late quartets, when he was totally deaf and cut off from the world."

Did they attempt an explanation of the *Grosse Fuge,* the most intimidating movement of all? Drucker laughs. "No, it's too long, and it's difficult to talk about, because without going into the technical definition of a fugue, you can't explain how Beethoven stretched that definition. We want to pull people in so that they'll be affected by the feeling and overwhelmed by the power of the music."

The current members have been together for more than two decades.

Setzer adds, "You can listen to the fugue as a sort of vision of the apocalypse without understanding a thing about it."

"I think there's another reason why the 'talking' CD is important," Finckel says. "People who listen mostly to popular music know something about the performers—in fact, sometimes too much: the way they look and dress, their personalities, their lives. But we classical musicians all look sort of alike because we dress the same way, and people never really hear from us. Making a kind of personal connection to the listener by using our own voices to express our thoughts brings us closer to the people who may not know us."

"Are there any?" I interrupt. They laugh and Finckel goes on, "This gives us a chance to further our status as ambassadors for this music. I feel one reason the Beethoven quartets are so great is that they are all so different. Each has something unique and wonderful, because, from the very first one, whatever Beethoven does is so *right*. One never gets tired of playing them; I always look forward to getting back to them after playing other things."

The American
String Quartet

The American String Quartet enters the new century celebrating its 25th anniversary. It has fulfilled the promise of its early, prize-winning years, logging untold miles on tours throughout the U.S. and abroad and developing a wide-ranging repertoire.

The four current players all studied at the Juilliard School in New York, where the quartet was formed in 1974. First violinist Peter Winograd was not one of the original members but joined in 1990, after studying with Dorothy DeLay and winning a top prize in the 1988 Naumburg International Violin Competition. Violinist Laurie Carney is a founding member of the quartet; she also studied with DeLay and earned both her B.M. and her M.M. at Juilliard. Violist Daniel Avshalomov was principal for the Brooklyn Philharmonia and the American Composers Orchestra, as well as the orchestras of the Spoleto, Tanglewood, and Aspen Festivals, before joining the ASQ. He was also a founding member of the Orpheus Chamber Ensemble. David Geber, cellist, studied principally with Ronald Leonard and Claus Adam and is a founding member of the quartet, as well as an active teacher and chair of the string department at the Manhattan School of Music.

In this interview, held in late 1993, the players discuss the quartet of Stradivari instruments they played on while recording the complete Mozart quartets, as well as their approach to the classic string-quartet repertoire and their affinity for contemporary music.

Mozart to Moderns

The American String Quartet, having won the Coleman Chamber Music Competition and the Walter W. Naumburg Chamber Music Award in 1974, made its New York debut at Alice Tully Hall that season and is celebrating its 20th anniversary with a concert in the same hall in May 1994. All four players come from families of musicians: cellist David Geber's parents are both cellists, his brother is principal cellist of the Cleveland Orchestra, and his wife is the cellist Julia Lichten. Violinist Laurie Carney's mother is a pianist, her father a music teacher; one of her several musician siblings is the concertmaster of the Royal Symphony Orchestra, and her husband is the cellist William Grubb. Violist Daniel Avshalomov's father and brother are composers and conductors, his mother is a singer and double-bass player, and his uncle, Max Felde, is the original violist of the La Salle String Quartet. Violinist Peter Winograd's father is the original cellist of the Juilliard String Quartet and his mother was a pianist.

The quartet has had several residencies. It was at the Mannes College of Music in New York from 1976 to 1980, then at the Peabody Conservatory in Baltimore from 1980 to 1990—which, Geber says, "was a wonderful association both for them and for us." This overlapped with the group's present residency at the Manhattan School of Music in New York, which began in 1984. At the Manhattan School, the quartet presents an annual concert series in addition to giving private lessons and coaching chamber music, mostly string quartets.

The members say the level of playing among the students is very high, but assembling the groups requires care and foresight. "Sometimes you have to try to match personalities as much as playing accomplishments, because we would all like a group to survive the year together," Carney explains. "We are getting better at this with experience.

"We've been conducting a summer program in Taos, New Mexico, since 1979, where we have to audition lots of kids coming from all over the world, and try to pick the best ones," Carney goes on. Each group spends two weeks preparing a piece for performance, working on it full time with no other commitments, for perhaps eight to ten hours a day.

"In the years we've been there," says Avshalomov, "They've done the Bartók Quartets, Alban Berg's Op. 3, the middle Beethovens, an occasional late Beethoven, and Mozart, the hardest of all."

Geber adds, "And what they accomplish in terms of learning how to prepare quickly and, as important, how to coexist with their peers in a very intense working situation, is worth its weight in gold."

By contrast, the students at the Manhattan School not only take a full curriculum, but they have to contend with all the distractions of life, and often also of making a living, in New York. However, they do study and perform a major work each semester, and, by dealing with musical and personal problems, they learn to "prepare themselves for meeting a lot of people in the music world whom they might not find compatible and still have to get along with," Carney says.

The players also conduct master classes. As chairman of the string department, Geber has a monthly class, "but though I throw it open to all the students to audit, I permit only my own students to play," he says. "I wouldn't want to make suggestions to other teachers' students that might be interpreted the wrong way. However, I also give master classes periodically in other places; I had one at the Cleveland Institute recently, for example. It's a very enjoyable facet of teaching, because you are only the good cop—in and out, very nonthreatening." How much good can one do in such a one-shot situation? "It's hard to say. You might plant an idea that has a good effect later, or reinforce something the regular teacher has been trying to get across."

Do they confer with the regular teachers beforehand? "Usually not," says Avshalomov. "I've tried to do that, but although it may have led me to say specific things, I found that I was denied my own first reactions, and that made the whole thing sort of stale for me. So now I prefer just to let the students play, and respond to what I hear and see."

Winograd adds, "The experience alone can be inspirational for the students."

The players try not to limit their activities entirely to the quartet, in spite of their very busy schedule performing as a group (in addition to their concerts at the Manhattan School and other locations in New York, they also travel on annual tours in both America and Europe). Each player frequently gives solo recitals at the school; as Carney comments, "I think it keeps our playing fresh in the quartet to go out and do different things."

Don Hunstein

Left to right, Peter Winograd, Laurie Carney, David Geber, and Daniel Avshalomov.

Winograd says, "I'm trying to keep up some of the solo playing I did before I joined the quartet. I have about five or ten concerto dates every year and also some recitals. And we're always looking for mutual projects. We've done programs where Laurie and Dan played the Mozart Sinfonia Concertante and David and I played the Brahms Double Concerto."

Geber also collaborates with recital partner Curt Cacioppo whenever possible. "He is a fine composer as well as a pianist. I've played two of his works and we're hoping to record one of them; it's a really wonderful piece."

The quartet's repertoire covers an enormous range, from classical to contemporary music. Having heard them many times in many different programs, I have long admired their stylistic versatility and sense of adventure, and I love their selfless commitment and genuine personal response to the music. Champions of contemporary works, their repertoire includes both Prokofiev quartets, which they have also recorded, and the complete quartets of Schoenberg. At their 20th-anniversary concert in May, they will premiere a quartet written for them by Kenneth Fuchs. They have commissioned and premiered works by a number of other American composers as well: Claus Adam, Thomas Oboe Lee, and the Fourth Quartet by George Tsontakis, all of which won the Kennedy Center's Friedheim Award.

What they play

Although the players recorded the complete Mozart quartets on the Axelrod quartet of instruments by Antonio Stradivari (see page 26), they normally use what Peter Winograd calls "wonderful instruments of our own." His violin was made by Giovanni Maria del Bussetto in Cremona in 1675. He used a Nikolaus Kittel bow at the time of this interview and now usually uses a François Tourte.

Laurie Carney's violin is a Carlo Tononi from Venice, 1763. She uses several bows; at the time of this interview she normally played with a Dominique Peccatte, but now she uses a Charles Bazin most of the time.

Daniel Avshalomov's viola was made by Andrea Amati in Cremona, 1568. He uses several bows, often changing them within a single program. At the time of this interview he primarily used one made by Jules Fétique, but now his choices include bows by Etienne Pajeot, Nicolas Maire, and Eugene Sartory.

David Geber's Cremonese cello was made by Giovanni Battista Ruggieri in 1667. He usually uses a bow by Nicolas Lupot.

The players use different strings on their own instruments than they used on the Strads, except for Carney, who uses Dominant G, D, and A and Goldbrokat E strings on both. Winograd currently uses a Eudoxa Oliv G, Dominant D and A, and Goldbrokat E on his own instrument, but on the Strad he used Eudoxa Olive label G, D, and A strings and a Goldbrokat E. Avshalomov uses Pirastro Wondertone Gold Label C, G, and D strings and a Larsen medium A on his own viola, and he played with a Dominant C, G, D, and Jargar A on the Strad. Geber used Dominants and Jargars on his own instrument at the time of this interview; now he uses a Spirocore Tungsten C and G and a Pirastro Permanente A and D. For the Strad, he used Eudoxa Gold label C, G, and D strings and a Jargar A.

"We've known Tsontakis since our school days," says Avshalomov, "and we always wanted to commission a piece from him. His style is in the friendlier category of contemporary music. There are themes, they are developed, the structure is fairly clear, and it's comprehensible and enjoyable. When we recorded his Fourth Quartet, we decided to couple it with his Third Quartet, so they have been released together." They do not play the other two. "He has said himself that he feels these, and especially No. 4, are stronger pieces," Avshalomov explains, "and we agree with him."

Claus Adam wrote his Quartet specifically for them. "It's a wonderful piece," says Geber. "His work as a composer was rather sporadic because of his performing career, but when he left the Juilliard Quartet [after 20 years as its cellist], he really began to write quite a lot: a cello concerto, a set of variations for orchestra, two piano sonatas, sketches for another quartet. It's wonderfully crafted music, very expressive, very original. I think that he would have been a major late–20th-century composer if he had lived longer. [He died in 1983.] But the quartet is a tough piece to program and take on tour, because the second half is in scordatura: each of us tunes two nonadjacent strings either up or down a semitone. So after you finish, the instruments keep going out of tune for the first 20 minutes of the next piece. But Adam was after a special effect: he wanted to have a tone-row—all the semitones—on the open strings. And he did it!"

"It creates an incredibly unusual sound," Carney adds.

At one of their concerts at the Manhattan School, I heard them play the first Charles Ives Quartet, which they say they like better than the second because it is more straightforward and tuneful. "I do think you have to be able to play music that doesn't enchant you in every detail, and of course the fault might lie with the player, not the music," says Avshalomov. "The Ives quartet represents a particular point in the development of American music, so whether we like it or not, it's fair to allow people to hear it from time to time and make their own decisions.

"People assume from our name that we play a great deal of American music," he continues, "but we don't. We did it more in the early days of the quartet, because we knew it was expected of us, but we soon began to recognize the risk of being perceived as specialists, as had happened with some other groups. Also, we had fewer concerts then; now, any work we offer may have to be repeated 30 or 40 times. This probably makes us more selective."

Geber adds, "there is such a wealth of good American music that we can afford to be discriminating." When I confess that the connection between their name and their repertoire had never occurred to me, they laugh. "Good! Keep it that way! We don't want to be labeled," says Geber with a smile.

If there was ever a danger of that, there certainly isn't any more. Some years ago, the group presented a cycle of the complete Beethoven quartets, a major undertaking in the career of any string quartet [they are performing that cycle again in the 1999–2000 season, along with contemporary American pieces]. They played the *Grosse Fuge* as the Finale of the Quartet, Op. 130, as Beethoven originally wrote it. However, it is frequently performed as a separate piece, because he later substituted a lighter movement. Geber says, "I think it's good either way. I love the Fugue; playing it is really a wonderful experience. On the other hand, the rest of that quartet is such an epic journey that it is nice to have the Rondo as a release."

Carney adds, "Of course, the Fugue is a thorny, difficult work, but we adore it. It's like mountain climbing; the final measures are so incredibly satisfying to play, I feel that it's come full circle."

They play a lot of Romantic music—Schubert, Brahms, Dvořák—and have also recorded two Dvořák quartets. They often invite guests for playing quintets with various instruments, most recently young pianists they met at the Van Cliburn Piano Competition, where, as successors to the Tokyo String Quartet, they were asked to collaborate in the chamber-music round. "Never in my life have I worked so hard," says Avshalomov with a laugh. "It felt as though we did more playing in eight days than ordinarily in half a season. We offered four piano quintets and four piano quartets, which the two violinists shared. We played with 12 pianists; some knew the music well, while others had never played chamber music before and didn't know how to give or take a cue, or to what or whom to listen for. Besides, we often played the same piece with several contestants and had to remember their different styles and ideas. We had decided among ourselves, ahead of time, that we would not attempt to act as teachers but simply go along with what the pianists wanted to do. Of course, if we sensed indecision, we might tip the balance one way or another. It was extremely hard work, but we discovered some very good players with whom we want to continue to collaborate, and we have already invited them to join us."

During the 1991–92 season, as part of the Mozart bicentennial, they performed the complete Mozart string quintets (one on each of six programs) with Michael Tree, the violist of the Guarneri String Quartet. "Many people put on all-Mozart programs that season," says Avshalomov, "but we thought it would be more interesting and enjoyable to build varied programs around the quintets, especially with Michael. We had been playing with him during the summer for many years, and fortunately he was available on all our dates." Discussing the C-Minor Quintet, which Mozart wrote first as a wind octet and then transcribed for five strings, we all agreed that we prefer the latter version for its warmer sound and greater expressive possibilities. "It's good to listen to the wind version occasionally," says Avshalomov, "so as to remember the original kinds of timbres and attacks that Mozart first heard. We've done a crossbred version with Heinz Holliger, the famous

Recordings

Adam: Quartet (CRI SD 478).

Dvořák: Quartet in D Minor, Op. 34, and Quartet in E-Flat Major, Op. 51; Schoenberg: String Quartet Concerto. New York Chamber Symphony, Gerard Schwarz, cond. (Nonesuch 9-79126).

Mozart: Quartets, K.428, K.589, K.157 (MusicMasters 67109).

Mozart: Quartets, K.421, K.387, K.171 (MusicMasters 67125).

Mozart: Quartets, K.499, K.159, K.575 (MusicMasters 67160).

Mozart: Quartets, K.168, K.172, K.590, K.458 (MusicMasters 67171).

Mozart: Complete String Quartets (MusicMasters 67194, 6 CDs).

Prokofiev: Quartet No. 1 in B Minor, Op. 50; Quartet No. 2 in F Major, Op. 92 (MHS 512302Z).

Tsontakis: Quartet No. 3, "Coraggio"; Quartet No. 4, "Beneath Thy Tenderness of Heart" (New World Records 80414).

oboist. He had a novel approach to the *maggiore* at the end of the last movement: he didn't think it was at all cheerful, but grim and rigid. I can still always see his terrible grimace when he said, 'This is not a smile, it's how a face looks when it's dead.'"

Asked whether he shares the complaint of many cellists that he is really playing a bassoon part, Geber smiles, "They just want to play in treble clef. I find it very gratifying, and it's beautifully written for the cello. The real challenge for me, with the oboe, was trying to blend the sonority, but I learned something about directness of articulation."

The 1991–92 concert series was notable not only for the scope of its programming, which ranged from Mozart to Schoenberg, and the admirable technical, musical, and expressive quality of the performances, but for introducing New York audiences to a remarkable set of instruments. "We've had the great good fortune to be loaned, from time to time, four Stradivaris which belong to Dr. Herbert Axelrod, the famous ichthyologist [fish expert]," says Avshalomov. The instruments are the 1687 "Ole Bull" and the 1709 "Greffuhle" violins, the "Marylebone" cello of 1688, and the 1695 "Herbert Axelrod" viola.

Don Hunstein

The players have busy schedules as soloists and teachers in addition to their quartet work.

"What makes them so extraordinary is that they are among the very few Strads that are decorated," says Avshalomov, "and that's why they were compiled as a set. The two violins were made for the King of Spain; he did not play himself, but hired people to play for him. In fact, the decorative inlay was a protective measure to make them physically distinctive, because these musicians would come to the castle hoping to switch their instruments for the king's when they left. Also, of course, all that ornamentation of ivory, ebony, and mother-of-pearl was deemed suitable for a king, as opposed to the ordinary civilian-model Strad."

Stradivari made perhaps less than a dozen decorated instruments altogether. "There's a viola," says Carney, "the so-called 'Oldham' Strad that's decorated more like the violins in Axelrod's quartet, in that the inlay around the top alternates between ivory and ebony." Only one Stradivari cello, the "Madrid," is known to have been decorated by the maker. In assembling his quartet, Axelrod commissioned luthier René Morel [then of Jacques Français Rare Violins] to apply decal copies of that decoration to this cello, the "Marylebone."

Since these four instruments were assembled into a set for their looks, how compatible are their sounds? "The sound is very lovely," says Geber. "And the sheer volume achievable with them is tremendous, greater, I find, than with many other instruments. The pleasure of being able to unleash this is quite a wonderful experience."

Winograd adds, "They are just so exhilarating and thrilling to play, as well as to look at."

Ordinarily, these instruments are kept at the Smithsonian Institution in Washington. "They've only been out perhaps three times during the last several years," says Carney. Knowing that it is essential, but always difficult, to get accustomed to another instrument, Axelrod allows the quartet to use his Strads for a couple of weeks before performances. The instruments are not loaned out to anyone else but stay on display at the Smithsonian. Asked if they find that people listen to the Strads more than to them, the players admit with a smile that there have been times when this seemed to happen.

Having contributed to the Mozart bicentennial by playing his quintets, the American String Quartet is celebrating its own 20th anniversary by recording the complete Mozart quartets for MusicMasters on the Axelrod Strads. The first volume is due to be released in November and will include one early and two late quartets. There will also be pictures of the instruments to give an idea of their singular beauty; their glorious sound, in the hands of these fine players, will speak for itself.

The Juilliard
String Quartet

The Juilliard String Quartet, one of America's best-known chamber-music groups, has traveled throughout the world, playing the classical repertoire and also championing contemporary composers. The group's long and successful association with the Juilliard School has brought them renown as teachers, and their commitment to coaching young chamber musicians comes through clearly in this 1989 interview. At the time, the quartet's members were founding first violinist Robert Mann, violinist Joel Smirnoff, violist Samuel Rhodes, and cellist Joel Krosnick. In late 1997, Mann retired and was replaced by Smirnoff; the second violinist now is Ronald Copes (who is second from the left in the photo opposite).

On Coaching and Performance

The Juilliard String Quartet was formed in 1946 as Quartet in Residence at the Juilliard School of Music, a position it still holds today. Meeting with its members for this interview brought back to me vivid memories of my own days at the school not too many years later, and one thing I remembered very well was how impressed I was to encounter four young, high-powered players just embarking on a high-powered career, who had decided to devote a large part of their time and energy to teaching and coaching chamber music. Participating in any of their classes, or just meeting them in the hallways of the school, one felt that they radiated the same vitality that they communicated in their concerts.

Thus it came as no surprise to me that in spite of several personnel changes over the years, I found them still full of a concentrated intensity and enthusiasm. Their taste in music is catholic; their knowledge—and not only of the string-quartet literature—is both wide and deep, and they speak about all aspects of it with an emphasis born of strong convictions and passionate involvement. As we talked about their coaching, it became clear that in the course of time they have witnessed many changes in teaching methods and attitudes, and their comments on the fact that much of the old authoritarian style has given way to a more open, tolerant approach was music to my ears. I suspect that they themselves might have been instrumental in bringing about some of these innovations.

I think it is fair to say that you are not only the first but perhaps the foremost coaching quartet in the field. Do you get your groups already formed or do you put them together?
RHODES A little of both.

Do you audition them first?
MANN Yes. All new students, whom we don't know, have to have an audition.

And if a group comes formed that doesn't seem to fit together, can you change it?
SMIRNOFF It'll usually self-destruct eventually.

MANN One doesn't like to impose too much if a group is really serious. If it's not serious, then one doesn't care whether one breaks it up or not.

How do you know if the players are serious?
MANN By the amount of work they do. They might not be so talented, but they may work very hard, and that group you cherish, as opposed to a lot of hot-shots who come together and practically *read* each week. They might seem to be playing very well, but they don't really get involved at all.

Are they all advanced players? And do they know much about playing quartets?
KROSNICK Sometimes you get somebody who doesn't play so well but has a background and knows quite a lot about chamber music, and sometimes you get a whole group who are brilliant instrumentalists but don't know anything about chamber music; they have a lot of trouble doing basic things like counting and playing with other people.

Do the groups tend to stay together for the four years?
SMIRNOFF Generally not. Occasionally there is a group that gets serious and develops into a real quartet.

MANN The Tokyo Quartet came here to study with us and they stayed together; the Emersons, too, and the American. [See stories on pp. 44, 6, and 18.]

Do you tell them what to study, or do they make their own choice?

RHODES It depends on the group and the amount of knowledge they have, and what any one of them has studied before. There are a number of considerations. I find I'm most successful when I give them at least a range, but let them choose. The repertoire is large enough; it doesn't matter where you start.

SMIRNOFF It's very important that they gain at least some literacy in the quartet repertoire. They should know how many quartets there are by Haydn, by Mozart, and so on, and what the possibilities are in this rich literature.

RHODES The area of greatest illiteracy, strangely enough, is the one where there should be the greatest literacy, and that is in the Haydn quartets. There are so many of them, and they are just not sufficiently known, not even the so-called "famous" ones. One thing I've tried to do this year is to have what amounts to supervised reading sessions, in which we go through any number of Haydn quartets so they get an idea of the range.

KROSNICK We should try to involve them in playing works written by their colleagues, the composers here, as well as other classical contemporary works, to involve them in the really fundamental act of creating as well as re-creating a performance. Then they can go back and realize that that's what they are supposed to be doing with a Haydn quartet also.

In the 1970s, quartet members (left to right) Robert Mann, Earl Carlyss, Joel Krosnick, and Samuel Rhodes.

Now suppose a new quartet comes to you, four people who have never played together or, in fact, played with anyone before. How do you help them to become a quartet?

RHODES You have to see specifically what the players are like individually, what their problems are together, what specific piece they choose. There are so many variables; it's very hard to answer that.

SMIRNOFF You know, some people are natural-born chamber players. They may not even know it, but they sit down and immediately they are able to play together. Of course, the art of chamber-music playing is the art of being able to produce something beautiful while you are listening very carefully to what's going on around you, and adapting to it and making changes on the spur of the moment, in time and pitch, and in terms of both technical and interpretive things. And there are some people who are just very good at this.

I seem to find that most people don't know how to listen, and that it's one of the most difficult things both to learn and to teach. So I ask this question every chance I get: How do you get students to learn how to listen?

KROSNICK It's not necessarily a musical question, you must under-stand.

Well, maybe not, but I think it's particularly applicable to music, because most people, especially if they are inexperienced, are so concerned with their own parts that they listen only to themselves.

KROSNICK It may be that you can point out to somebody that they are not listening, or show them techniques of listening.

Yes, what are some of those?

KROSNICK Well, there are all kinds of analytic tools in music that show people how to listen. Melodic lines, how they are made up harmonically, the harmonic rhythm of a line, how impulses are created musically. Of course, you may discover that you can teach somebody all kinds of diag-nostic tools, and they will still not be able to apply them.

SMIRNOFF I think one thing that comes into play, in addition to a per-son's sensitivity, is physical coordination. Now in sports, the concept of many things going on at one time, even if it's only in your own body, has already been instilled. So the idea of coordination is very important and has to be communicated, and if anybody has the experience of being able to do a bunch of things at once, then they are already on the road to understanding what it is to coordinate with someone else. And of course, at its most basic, we're talking about the ability to feel pulse together, to feel tempo together, to be able to communicate pulse to each other even without playing. That's especially difficult in a slow-moving piece where nothing is happening. And another basic thing is the ability to hear true pitch.

Are there any exercises you can give people for intonation?

SMIRNOFF I always tell my students to orient toward the fourths and fifths. You want to get the perfect intervals first; they are kind of the bones of the harmonic structure, and then you can tune in the more transitory notes around those.

RHODES Regarding intonation, there are two standard situations that you come across in various combinations. One is the unison, which you have to practice with one technique, and the other is the chordal pas-sage, which demands another technique. How does one go about clean-ing up the unisons? I think we all go over very carefully what to listen for; we try to shade the pitches all in the same direction according to the tonal function of the notes, so at least the fingers are all aiming the same way.

MANN Actually, wouldn't you say there is a kind of ongoing difference of approach between two attitudes toward intonation in a quartet? I know that the old Hungarian Quartet believed in and taught the tem-pered scale the way a piano tuner tunes the piano. So such things as leading tones, whether they be the seventh or the third, were generally played pretty accurately and straightforwardly, the theory being that if everybody always aimed in the same place, intonation problems would lessen. We, on the other hand, generally adhere to the more expressive attitude, which is more medieval, too: We want to keep our tones in relationship to each other.

RHODES We string players are lucky to have the ability to be fluid with that kind of thing, and not to make commitments one way or another. One of our goals is to get students to develop the sensitivity and control to be able to deal with that.

KROSNICK I've discovered that the great string players, whether consciously or not, really have the kind of intonation that has something to do with a very expressive perception of what the pitches mean to them. I heard an example one day on the radio: the slow movement of the Tchaikovsky Violin Concerto, played by Milstein and then by Heifetz. Milstein's very tempered intonation and Heifetz' very leading-tone intonation were really something. There are all sorts of things in the bow approach and the vibrato approach that are *very* different and highlight each player's whole approach to the piece, starting with how the pitches and harmonies are perceived. Intonation is much more than some sort of good behavior.

Andrew Ritchie

Joel Krosnick at a master class at the San Francisco Conservatory.

If somebody can't play with the intonation necessary to unify them in the C-Minor Brahms Quartet, let's say, it's possible they just don't understand C minor. One of the things we've been doing here the last several years, and that we also did in our residency at Michigan State, is to rehearse in public about once a month, and we are not hesitant at all about taking something that we're working on and playing through it slowly, fixing pitches, talking about it: "Are we doing leading tones in this passage or are we trying to play tempered?" And then we'll turn around and explain to the students that it depends on the harmonic attitude. If we are not leaning in the same direction, we are in trouble.

Sounds like the perfect breeding ground for disagreement.

MANN Oh yes; the first quarrel in an inexperienced quartet often is, "*You* are too high; *you* are too low."

But intonation cannot be the only thing a quartet needs to become unified.

RHODES No, of course; just to unify the sound you have to use the same type of tone quality, the same amount of vibrato or lack of vibrato, bow pressure . . .

What they play

When the Juilliard Quartet plays at the Library of Congress, the members use four Cremonese instruments made by Antonio Stradivari; they were all given to the Library in 1936 by Gertrude Clarke Whittall. As the institution's quartet in residence, the Juilliard is the only group allowed to play on these instruments. Before it took over the post in 1962, the Budapest Quartet, itself in residence at the Library for 22 years, played on the Stradivaris.

In addition to the unusual instruments discussed beginning on p. 39, the members of the Juilliard all have their own instruments for all other occasions. Violinist Joel Smirnoff (second from left in the photo below) plays on a Giuseppe Guarneri ("Joseph filius Andreae"). Current second violinist Ronald Copes (not pictured below) plays a Nicola Amati from 1676. His bow is by Lupot, and he uses Dominant strings with a Pirastro Olive Goldstahl E string. Samuel Rhodes plays a Brescian viola made by Peregrino Zanetto, ca. 1600. His bow is by Morizot and he uses Jargar and Dominant strings. Joel Krosnick's cello is also a Guarneri "filius Andreae," from 1721. His bow is a James Tubbs and he uses Jargar and Thomastik Spirocore strings.

SMIRNOFF . . . and then to create a mood, an atmosphere with each other, which is somehow shared.

Well, what do you do with a quartet where the members disagree about interpretation? Suppose a fairly advanced student quartet is studying a piece and they all want to do it differently. Do you step in as umpires, or what do you do?

RHODES A group has to have quite a bit of sophistication to get to that level, so the disagreements I find are much more fundamental than musical. Personalities clash in all sorts of funny ways; outside factors like scheduling, people coming late to rehearsals, that sort of nonsense. But to get people with real musical disagreements—I'd welcome a group like that.

KROSNICK There is one thing we do ourselves and I certainly recommend it. If there are three ways, three very different approaches, I simply tell the students: "*You* have the floor, *you* have the floor, *you* have the floor, and you prepare the three different ways of dealing with the problem." We ourselves turn to each other and say: "Tell you what, *you* run the rehearsal now, tell us what to do, let's build it your way." Fine, we might fix that up and say, "OK, who's got another way?" We even went into performance once with two ways of doing the Minuet of the Mozart G-Minor Viola Quintet, and Bobby [Mann] turned to us and said, "Which way are we doing this tonight?"

MANN The backdrop for this discussion is the fact that something significant has happened in the musical world vis-à-vis, say, a century ago, when, a little bit like religion and the concept of God and the universe, musicians used to feel they *knew* the right solution or the right interpretation. For example, Toscanini had his own way, and that could not be challenged by anybody. Today there is a more pluralistic concept of everything; whereas one musician might have felt, "This is the only way I can play something," today, I think, one loves to feed off *many* ways of playing something. Just take even the business of early music: you've got people playing Haydn with modern instruments and modern concepts, with early instruments and early concepts, and people trying to bridge the gap. You have to accept many ideas.

Yes, and that is good. When I was going to Juilliard, the idea was that the teacher absolutely knew and his way was the only way. I had not been brought up like that and it bothered me. I was a little older than most of the other students and it was very hard for me to adjust.

KROSNICK I also studied with someone who taught chamber music at Juilliard, and that person would say—it was the most adamant thing I'd ever heard—"You don't have to do it that way, but while you're here in this room, you do it my way." And that was considered liberal at that time. But you'd be surprised—if two different ways are really rehearsed and realized, the disagreements, many of which may just be contentious disagreements of personality, may flatten out. People may suddenly realize, "Wait a minute, I actually *like* it that way." Or, "OK, I like it, all except one idea." And what's really news is when somebody who is a proponent of one way sits back and suddenly realizes, "I don't like it." And in helping them get through that, we really show them how to conduct such an argument.

What do you do when people have personal fights, if they otherwise seem to fit together and you don't want to just let the group fall apart?

RHODES Sometimes you can help resolve it just by talking it out. It really depends, again, on how deep-seated the problem is. There are cases where you can't do anything.

MANN I had a quartet that literally seemed to have a *terrible* problem, and all of a sudden it became clear why: One of them spoke English with a Japanese accent, and another with a French-Canadian accent, neither of which I could understand. They had difficulties understanding *anything*, let alone an *idea*.

On the other hand, I now have another quartet in which all four are from Germany.

That's good, at least they can all speak German to each other.

MANN And they do, in front of me.

KROSNICK I've had a group come to me and say, "Look, we don't like so-and-so; can you get rid of him for us?" And I said, "Why don't we sit down together and you tell that person what you don't like and let that person answer you?" And I've had that person say, "I had no idea you felt that way; why didn't you tell me?" So I feel one of the things we should do here is try to show students that, though this is music, it's also practice in human relations.

I once wound up saying to a group in Tanglewood, "You'd better enjoy playing the Schubert Quintet together, because you may never get to play it again." And they all said, "Why is that?" "Because you can't play the Schubert Quintet alone. Even if you practice, you can't play any of this music alone." I mean, we ourselves get a tremendous amount back from all the vigorous, difficult things we are always talking about together. You can't play the Beethoven cycle unless there are four of you. So we have to admit to students, "Look, I put together a bunch of groups before I got one where I could actually go through the complexity of expressing myself, of listening to somebody else, of forgiving and being forgiven."

And when students say, "Ah, the hell with it, I don't want it," I say, "Do you know that's an awfully large thing you're saying you don't want? It means, either I play alone, or in such a large, anonymous group that I will pretend I don't care about it."

Now suppose you get a really good group that's on a level of sophistication where one can talk about interpretation, and suppose they have an idea which they don't know how to realize. How do you help them to do it? How, in fact, do you help a group rehearse effectively by themselves?

RHODES When they play for you, you can hear the seeds of the idea, and you can tell if it's undeveloped, or going in a certain way, and you can suggest and guide them in a certain direction and let them take it from there and develop it their own way. All of us, in any given piece of the repertoire, have been through hundreds and thousands of ideas, and we can pick them all out.

MANN There are two levels to that, too. One is where you have spent a great part of your life absorbing all the people you respect and love who've been involved in music, and therefore you know a kind of compounded tradition and anti-tradition about a piece and its background and history and so on. But there is also another approach that I've become more and more interested in as time goes on, and that is how to sharpen the tools of inquiry and involvement of young people dealing with materials in which they are, after all, not beginners. I mean, they've been playing notes for a long time, they've been playing instruments for a long time, and they've been playing various composers for a long time; how do you sharpen their perceptions about what those pieces are made of, how they came to be created? That is a way of releasing the imagination.

Left to right, Robert Mann, Joel Smirnoff, Samuel Rhodes, Joel Krosnick.

And a far cry from just telling them what to do.

MANN And I also find that with most—I won't say with all, but with most—serious young students, one has to psychologically push them to test extremes, because you can never understand, say, a tempo character, unless you *really* know what is too fast and have experienced it, or know what is too slow and have experienced it. You can't just say, "This is the right tempo, or let's find the right tempo somewhere in the center of the world."

How far do you go in striving to perfect something?

RHODES The best way to get them to perfect something is to have them prepare for a performance, even if it's only one movement. I also sometimes have them play for one of my colleagues, for a different point of view; it throws a new light on a piece they've been working on.

MANN I've had lots of fun with some of the less-experienced groups, saying, "Let's not learn *all* these pieces perfectly; let's just go through, say, the three Brahms quartets in a semester, so that by the time it's finished, you'll know that body of the literature." I feel that all those who play in orchestra should not learn just specific pieces for the glory of the school and its concerts, but that they should, when they get out of school, know all the Beethoven symphonies.

I wish somebody had thought of that when I was here. I felt we never had a chance to get acquainted with the literature.

KROSNICK Something happened to each of us, in our chamber-music experience, that rarely happens now with all the busy stuff going on in conservatories. Every Friday night, you played chamber music with your teacher. My parents were amateur musicians, I grew up in New Haven, and all the Yale graduate students and all kinds of professionals used to come to our house. By the time I was 12 or 13, I was preparing certain pieces and after a while I had enough knowledge of the literature to be able to actually sit down and sight-read things with people regularly. All of us had those experiences where we played great, great amounts of the repertoire. The kids nowadays very rarely do that.

MANN It's one of the significant differences between today and, say, 30 or 20 years ago. In my day, all of us were always rushing around trying to organize evenings to read music. We didn't have as many concerts to go out and play in the professional world. So we were just reading and reading.

SMIRNOFF But I think the whole idea that it was also a social occasion doesn't exist anymore. When I was playing the Haydn quartets with my friends, we would play four or five quartets a night, and then there would be a long discussion afterwards, not about the music, but about baseball and everything else.

KROSNICK It was one of the real means for people who studied music to have a social life. I am always very sorry that somehow we haven't been able to be catalysts for today's kids, but it's very hard. These kids are trying to pay the rent, they're taking jobs, they are having a professional life while they're studying here; the school keeps them fantastically busy, and they don't read chamber music, basically. Very rarely do we have people come in to audition who really have a knowledge of the literature—maybe one in every 20. It used to happen once in a while that somebody came in and you said, "Do you know any Beethoven quartets?" And that person would say, "Which one would you like to hear?"

MANN This is the century of the virtuoso. Nowadays, there are more kids who come to Juilliard offering to play a Paganini caprice, and when one asks, "Which one?" they say, "Which one would you like?"

So then you have to integrate these virtuosos into a chamber group. No wonder you are grateful when one of the opposite sort walks in.

[Author's note: A few days before the interview, at the 92nd Street YMHA, the Juilliard Quartet played Bach's Die Kunst der Fuge in their own

arrangement. This differs significantly from other string-quartet versions which, since the alto voice often goes below the violin G string and the tenor below the viola C, break the voice-leading by transposing certain notes up an octave or shifting them to other instruments. In order to play all the notes exactly as they appear in Bach's open score, Smirnoff alternated between violin and viola, while Rhodes used an unusually large viola, which he commissioned from luthier Marten Cornelissen. It is tuned to D, G, C, G, low enough to encompass the range of the tenor line.]

Your performance was splendid. So now I'm full of questions about the Bach. Are you the first ones who are doing it in this particular layout?

KROSNICK Actually, our relationship with it started with a request that we play the Roy Harris transcription on our series at the Library of Congress. But we don't like it and we said, "No, no, if we're going to do it, why don't we start with the *Neue Bach-Ausgabe* and go from there?" Originally we had to switch notes a lot in the lines, but then Sam [Rhodes] came up with the idea of the lowered viola, so now there's everything from two violins, lowered viola, and cello to violin, viola, lowered viola, and cello. That way you'll get all the pitches of the original in the right order.

I saw from the score that Bach tells you even less than usual—no tempos, no phrase marks, no articulation. Since you had to decide all those things for yourselves, how did you do it?

RHODES There are a number of things you can go by, like a knowledge of the style, where and how particular sections fit into the whole, what pattern you feel is made by going from one to the next, and when the tempo starts to move.

Former first violinist Robert Mann retired from the quartet in 1997 but is still an active player and coach.

How do you decide about the articulation?

RHODES One of the most important things is to differentiate the material in order to express the counterpoint. This becomes crucial, I think, in the multiple fugues. In a fugue with three subjects, it's important for the listener to be able to distinguish them when they're played in various combinations. We try to use something inherent in the music itself to do that. One subject may be played more staccato, another with a lot of emotional affects, so when they all come together it's not chaotic; each of the three can be picked out because of their very separate characters. To help the articulation, we use two Baroque bows and two transitional bows.

Recordings

Babbitt: *Quartet No. 4; Sessions: Quartet No. 2; Wolpe: Quartet (CRI 587).*

Bach: *The Art of the Fugue (Sony Classical 45937).*

Beethoven: *The Complete String Quartets (CBS 37873).*

Beethoven: *Quartets, Opp. 18, 59, 74, and 75 (CBS 37868 and 37869).*

Brahms: *Quartets Nos. 1–3; Clarinet Quintet. With C. Neidich, clarinet (Sony 66285).*

Brahms: *String Quintets Nos. 1, 2. With W. Trampler, viola (Sony 68476).*

Carter: *String Quartets Nos. 1–4 (Sony 47229).*

Debussy: *Quartet; Dutilleux: Ainsi la nuit; Ravel: Quartet (Sony 52554).*

Dvořák: *Quartet No. 12; Piano Quintet, Op. 81. With R. Firkušný, piano (Sony 8170).*

Fine: *String Quartet (CRI 574).*

Franck: *String Quartet; Haydn: The Seven Last Words of Christ. With Benita Valente, soprano; Jan DeGaetani, mezzo-soprano; Jon Hemphrey, tenor; Thomas Paul, baritone (Sony 44914).*

Hindemith: *String Quartets Nos. 3, 5 (Wergo 6283).*

Kuhlau: *Flute Quintets. With Jean-Pierre Rampal, flute (CBS 44517).*

Lerdahl: *First String Quartet; Martino: String Quartet (CRI 551).*

Mozart: *String Quartets Nos. 14–19 (Odyssey 45826).*

Mozart: *String Quintets (Odyssey 45827).*

Prokofiev: *Overture on Hebrew Themes. With Giora Feidman, clarinet; Yefim Bronfman, piano (Sony 58966).*

Schoenberg: *Verklärte Nacht. With Walter Trampler, viola; Yo-Yo Ma, cello (Sony 47690).*

Schubert: *The Complete String Quartets, Nos. 12–15 (Odyssey 45617).*

Schubert: *String Quartets Nos. 12, 14 (Odyssey 42602 and Sony 46343).*

Schubert: *String Quintet, D.956. With B. Greenhouse, cello (CBS 42383).*

Sibelius: *String Quartet, Op. 56; Verdi: String Quartet (Sony 48193).*

Smetana: *String Quartet No. 1 (Sony 63302).*

Now what about this extraordinary instrument you use? Why is the lowest string tuned to G, not F?

RHODES Well, that's just my way of doing it. The lowest note called for is a G, and even though the instrument is very large, I don't want it to have to go any lower than necessary.

Isn't it difficult to finger this way?

RHODES Well, I just write it in.

And your arrangement requires a second violinist who is able and willing to switch to viola . . .

SMIRNOFF Willing, anyway . . .

KROSNICK The thing that awes me is that he comes out on the stage and he plays the viola *alone* at the start.

Well, it certainly all sounds very authentic. I have other questions about authenticity. I remember you gave a series of concerts of the complete Mozart String Quartets and Quintets. In the D-Major Quintet—

CHORUS —we play the chromatic in the last movement. That's the way he originally wrote it.

Where did you find it?

RHODES In the new Bärenreiter *Complete Works*. Not only is it there in the body of the edition, but it has a picture of the manuscript on the first page and you can see quite clearly that the original way he wrote it was the descending chromatic scale. Later on, it's an ascending chromatic scale. And it's been changed in a foreign hand, to the way that you probably know it.

Which edition do you generally use for Mozart?

RHODES We use the Bärenreiter scores for reference for the quintets. For the quartets, it's a combination.

MANN [Musicologist] Alfred Einstein is, to me, the real savior of Mozart, because he notes, in his very extensive scores, the manuscript and first edition differences, and points out what Mozart did between the two, and that really gives you as much of a Bible connection as you can get with Mozart.

What about that F-flat in the viola in the slow movement of the E-Flat Quintet?

MANN You don't like that note?

It sounds so wrong!

RHODES That may be, but if you look at the manuscript, it's very clear that it's the correct note.

Then there is that bar in the slow movement of the "Dissonant" Quartet, where the question is: Should the 16ths start alone for awhile, or should there be eighths in the other parts? It occurs several times, and they are not all the same.

KROSNICK That's right; of the three times, two should start alone.

Let me ask you about Beethoven. When you play the complete quartets—

SMIRNOFF —in six concerts—

KROSNICK —we play Op. 130 twice, once with the Fugue and, at another point in the series, with the other Finale. It changes the entire work. What's very interesting about the Grand Fugue *and* the Rondo is that they both parallel the first movement, harmonically as well as in terms of length and types of material. They are both written to balance that piece and they both fulfill that purpose. A less-than-huge last movement could not have done it, and that Rondo is *enormous.*

Tell me about your American repertoire.

MANN Well, you know that we are doing the Eighth Quartet by George Perle. We've done all the Carter Quartets, and we'd like very much to do all four during one year.

KROSNICK We are also involved with the Richard Wenick Quartet, the Davidowski Quartet, which we commissioned, the Stefan Wolpe Quartet, and I think we are all proud of our involvement with this ongoing history. But over the years it's been very difficult to find sponsor concert groups that are willing to let us play these pieces. We put attractive, saleable programs around them, but a lot of times sponsors, who are quite realistically concerned about selling out their series, will pick the program without the challenge. So we try to put Carter on one, Wolpe on another, something else on a third, to see to it that people will know we're serious about wanting them to go on an adventure with us. And we want to record this music, it's music we believe in—but often it's not commercially feasible. So we've had trouble recording all of our major American 20th-century repertoire, and we hope and wish there will be increasingly viable ways.

MANN There is one significant development in the Juilliard Quartet's history that I'd like to mention. It's a good one and a serious one. In the early days, we used to play lots of new music; it was not unusual for us to learn 10–15 new works in a year. But what did that really mean? It meant that we would learn them hurriedly—with all our resources at hand, of course, but still, rather superficially—perform them once or twice, and then not play them again. Today there are many other groups who are playing music of this nature, too, so we learn fewer works, but we learn them much more carefully. And we program them as regular concert pieces, so that a difficult work gets not just one or two performances, but, like the Milton Babbit Fourth—how many times did we play that?

RHODES Over a whole season, and then, I think, part of another one.

MANN So it got about two dozen performances or more. We not only play it better, we learn it more deeply, and the world at large becomes much more aware of a very fine work finely performed, and that is a definite improvement.

KROSNICK When we start to play it with the kind of lucidity and relaxation with which we invest a classical work, that's when we really feel on top of it.

That takes a long time, doesn't it?

RHODES A very, very long time, yes.

KROSNICK You can't exactly say that we under-stand, say, the Fourth Carter when we undertake it. We understand it, we have enough experience in the grammar to know that there is something in there, and we go in after it. And we start shar-ing it with audiences hoping we will be much bet-ter re-creators of, for example, the Babbitt, the Martino, and the Fourth Carter at the end of our relationship with them than at the beginning.

Surely that's how it should be—if it were the other way, then that would be terrible!

MANN I know certain people who are whizzes; they can read every-thing. But then, if they keep practicing anything very long, it gets worse.

The current lineup, left to right: Joel Smirnoff, Ronald Copes, Joel Krosnick (in front), and Samuel Rhodes.

There seems to be no danger of that here.

MANN Well, we feel we're in good shape, as long as health lasts, and we're having a good time.

The Tokyo String Quartet

The Tokyo String Quartet, as most chamber-music lovers know, is that extraordinary group that has successfully transcended national and cultural barriers—first as four native Japanese playing Western classical music, and then by inviting a Canadian to join them when their first violinist returned to Japan. Founded in 1969 and now internationally acclaimed, the group tours regularly throughout Japan, Europe, and North America, and celebrated its 25th anniversary by performing the complete Beethoven quartets worldwide. It also serves on the faculty of the Yale School of Music and the related Norfolk Chamber Music Festival, and gives regular master classes at the University of Cincinnati College-Conservatory of Music.

Since this 1987 interview, the Tokyo has seen several changes. Its longtime first violinist, Peter Oundjian, left the group because of a strained hand; Mikhail Kopelman, formerly of the Borodin String Quartet (see page 58), took his place in 1996. In 1999, cellist Sadao Harada resigned and was replaced by Clive Greensmith.

The Power of Four

A t this interview, the four players—violinists Peter Oundjian and Kikuei Ikeda, violist Kazuhide Isomura, and cellist Sadao Harada—explored with me a wide range of musical subjects. They talked with complete candor and spontaneity about a generous variety of intricate technical and musical concerns, giving me a rare glimpse of the inner workings of a string quartet on and off the stage. Yet despite the seriousness of intent and subject matter, the atmosphere was friendly and relaxed, the discussion frequently punctuated by bursts of laughter.

Much has been written about your being living proof that music is truly a universal language. May I suggest that we sketch in the background lightly and then go on to musical matters?

IKEDA We started out with four Japanese, which is unique in the Western music world. If you are German or French or Italian, you have a historical, traditional concept of the music and may take certain things for granted. We are not like that; we tend to want to know very precisely what we want to do and be very careful about details.

ISOMURA We started out with similar backgrounds. We studied in Japan at the Toho School of Music with Professor Hideo Saito, who had a very profound influence on us. When we came to New York, we studied at Juilliard with the Juilliard Quartet [see page 28] and they were a strong influence, especially [violinist] Robert Mann and [violist] Raphael Hillyer. We loved the way they played the classical repertoire and we especially loved their Bartók and the new Viennese music.

And another thing: from the beginning, the main reason we played quartets is that all four of us are so crazy about that great literature. To us, the love of that music always comes first. Rather than try to play more beautifully than someone else, we just try to do it justice. So we always knew it was very important to unify our style, our expression. Even if each of us had a good musical personality, if we all headed in different directions, we would never have a great personality as a group.

You certainly have that. How do four first-class string players transform themselves into one first-class string quartet? One can listen to four great players sit down and play together and it's nice, but it's not a quartet.

OUNDJIAN It takes a long time to achieve this unity. You have to have four instruments that are not too brilliant or abrasive or individual-sounding. It takes a very specific kind of playing, maybe a specific kind of person, too. You have to have a certain kind of containment, and you have to develop the tremendous joy of playing with somebody else and making a sound that you know is coming out as one thing. Very often, you must resist the instinct that says, "I want to be heard now, this is my line." We don't really want the people in the audience to say, "That cellist is amazing." We'd rather have them say, "That quartet!" So a certain kind of approach and a certain kind of person really go hand in hand.

How does one rehearse for that, technically?

OUNDJIAN It involves the most basic things, but it can also be very subtle. For example, if four of you are playing a big chord—big, round chords should sound like a big orchestra, very bold and full, but never forced. If among the four of us the weight of the bow, the speed of the bow, the connection between bow and vibrato are almost identical, then we're going to get a really powerful, unified sound. If one person is vibrating a little too fast, or is trying to create a very individual intensity, the decibel level may be higher, but that great quartet-weight sound will be lacking.

And there's something else: We have to feel, before we even begin, that we want to hear the same kind of thing. We don't have one guy going, "Here, there's the lead, now you guys play." We know exactly what's happening among the four of us from the moment we sit down and everyone concentrates on the music and our bows go up in the air. We can really sense each other—we could close our eyes and, without even thinking, start almost identically together.

IKEDA We also talk about the need to match vibrato, not just to create a beautiful quartet sound but a particular quality—some intensity, maybe.

OUNDJIAN Yes, the vibrato is important not only for the sound, but for the intonation as well. This is what I find so interesting: even though we play together constantly, we can never stop being aware of this, especially since we play so much different repertoire. Otherwise our vibratos start going in different directions.

Christian Steiner

In 1996, left to right, Sadao Harada, Kazuhide Isomura, Mikhail Kopelman, and Kikuei Ikeda.

IKEDA It is very important to be able to listen, whether you are playing or not. The second violin is not that difficult—you can play the notes—but you have to be able to listen to the different parts, including your own, all the time. When we rehearse, it helps the intonation and ensemble when one of us is not playing, only listening. But you have to develop a critical ear, or you may not hear what is happening precisely.

ISOMURA We are constantly criticizing each other in rehearsal. We are very open, very straight. For example, when we are talking about pitch, if somebody is flat, we tell him right away. And actually, while you are playing, you are not always the best judge of intonation or other things. We should always watch each other with our eyes, our ears. Some people cannot take the criticism, even if they are fantastic players and really want to play string quartet.

OUNDJIAN Yes, criticism can be painful. Any of us might get into a bad habit, and then somebody has to have the courage to say so. For example, when I first joined the quartet, I used to vibrate above the pitch, because I thought that to become a great soloist, that was the thing to do. In fact, I was wrong, and many of the great teachers have taught students to vibrate below the pitch. Kazu [Isomura] was the first one to notice and to have the courage to say, "You know, you could try to practice pulling your vibrato back. It's not that you're putting your fingers down too high, but when you vibrate, it sounds high." So for six years, I've been working on getting my vibrato to come right in. One of

What they play

The Tokyo Quartet performs on the "Paganini" Quartet, a group of instruments made by Antonio Stradivari and named for the virtuoso Nicolò Paganini, who bought and played them during the 19th century. The violins date from 1680 and 1727, the viola was made in 1731, and the cello is from 1736. The instruments were loaned to the Tokyo by the Nippon Music Foundation in 1995, when it purchased them from the Corcoran Gallery of Art in Washington, D.C. In prior years the group played on a quartet of instruments by Nicola Amati dating from 1656–77, also then owned by the Corcoran Gallery.

The members also have their own instruments. Mikhail Kopelman's violin is a 1718 Stradivari. He uses Helicore strings and his bow is a Sartory. Kikuei Ikeda's violin is a Lorenzo Storioni from 1778. He uses Dominant strings with a Westminster E, and his bow is by Nicholas Eury. Kazuhide Isomura's 17th-century viola was by Antonio Mariani, and he uses a Jargar A string, a Helicore D, and a Thomastik Dominant G and C. His bow is by Pajeot. Clive Greensmith's cello was made in 1992 by Peter and Wendy Moes, and he uses Jargar A and D strings and Pirastro Permanent G and C strings. His bow is by Emile Ouchard.

Christian Steiner

our most important values is that in order to be individuals, we've got to sound unified. When we do, we can relax and be ourselves, and I think that's the key to great quartet playing. You're not trapped with three other people, you're making something together that is very free.

For example, everybody knows that attacks should be together. What people classically neglect is cutoffs, and not just at the end of a piece, a phrase, or a chord. For example, if you're going into a sforzando and you want some weight behind it, you want to have a little release and you may want to re-attack.

IKEDA If you don't listen very carefully, you might not notice, because it happens in a split second, but if you are together as a unit all the time, it creates a much more powerful message.

OUNDJIAN That's right; with four people, things are not just four times better, they're 16 or 100 times better. It's not even something the ear can necessarily identify, but the power of it will go straight beneath the skin and to the heart.

Let's talk a bit about balance. How do you bring out more and less important lines?

OUNDJIAN No line is ever unimportant—

IKEDA —only subordinate.

Isn't it difficult to tell, while you're playing, whether anyone is too loud or too soft?

ISOMURA Whenever we play a concert, we have a rehearsal in the concert hall. For us, the hall is like an instrument and it is important to try out its acoustics.

But with people in the hall, it won't be the same anyway.

OUNDJIAN The sound will dry out, but its character is very unlikely to change. And it's good to warm up. Say you've been playing in a lot of very resonant, beautiful, warm-sounding halls, and you come to a town where the hall is very dry and shrill and unpleasant. If you spend an hour getting adjusted it'll prevent you from charging your way through the concert, instinctively wanting to fill in the gaps because there's no resonance. You'll start playing faster and you'll sound as if you want to get out of there, which you well may.

How do you choose your repertoire?

ISOMURA In our early days, we used to play a lot of Classical repertoire, and quite a bit of Bartók and other contemporary composers, under the influence of the Juilliard Quartet. And we had a reputation for being very good at that, so we didn't have much chance to play the big Romantic pieces or anything unusual. Later, shortly before our original first violinist [Koichiro Harada] left, we started to play more

Romantic repertoire, and even more since Peter joined. I think it gave us a chance to open up some new avenues.

How long does it take to learn a new work or a new program?

HARADA It depends. Really, never very long. At the beginning of our career it took much longer. For example, we would play Beethoven. How many Beethoven quartets had we experienced then? Maybe two. But after we had played 14, to prepare another one with Peter was a little bit easier. We already knew the style.

That brings us to the question of style—both the composer's and your own.

OUNDJIAN Yes, the way you develop your playing style is absolutely crucial.

ISOMURA I think at the beginning our style was really quite Classical. It had to do with playing mostly that repertoire. We tried to respect the authenticity of the music and had very unified ideas about its interpretation. That also gave us a very clean ensemble.

OUNDJIAN But as to style in terms of musical taste. . . . You know, there's a lot of very aggressive music making going on nowadays, and it doesn't matter what the music may be. You hear aggressive Mozart, which is fine; I have nothing against it as long as I don't have to play it like that. But for us, I think we have a genuine instinct to play with a more traditional, European approach. Is that fair to say? We don't try to make tremendous excitement or tremendous intensity, we don't put neon lights over things. Obviously, that's not to everyone's taste; some people say, "Oh, it's so pristine, it's without real depth, it's cold." Well, to us, the opposite would probably sound vulgar.

Another problem is capturing a tempo.

OUNDJIAN I believe you often have to think of something other than tempo. You've got to capture this very special mood and do it with the sound, and then the tempo will take care of itself.

I sometimes think people tend to play fast in order to sound brilliant.

OUNDJIAN   Yes, but sometimes the faster you play, the less brilliant it sounds. People tend to confuse tempo with tempo character, when they are really two quite different things. We spend a lot of time working on how to get character changes without messing around with the tempo too much. In other words, a crescendo doesn't have to get faster; it might in fact want to get slower, or at least feel like that. Conversely, you can learn to get a feeling of relaxation purely by doing a diminuendo without slowing down.

You can even do exercises for this. Let's say we want to grow in intensity here. In the actual performance, we'll probably get faster from the beginning of the passage to the climax, but in order to practice doing that in a very subtle way, let's try once to get slower all the way through the passage to the climax and create intensity by expanding the tempo. That kind of exercise can be very good for your musical vocabulary. You should be able to do all kinds of things, musically speaking, so that if you get stuck in the wrong tempo one day in a concert, you can do something about it. There's nothing more ridiculous than being in the middle of a passage and saying, "Isn't this too fast?" or, "What speed did we start at?" A tempo has to be allowed to evolve, but in general, to me, the music takes on a much stronger stature when there are no obvious changes in the tempo.

Do you feel that your interpretation of works that you've been playing for a long time has changed over the years? I was wondering specifically whether the fact that you are now playing more Romantic music has affected the way you approach the Classical repertoire.

OUNDJIAN Actually, that's quite a danger.

HARADA I think it is possible to make Haydn, for example, too rich, too thick. Sometimes we say, "We never used to play like this, we made it simpler," and maybe that is because we play a lot of Romantic music now.

Former first violinist Peter Oundjian left the quartet because of a hand injury and has turned to conducting.

OUNDJIAN You can easily fall into the trap of going for this nice "rich" sound. But that Romantic style doesn't really work for Haydn or Mozart—not for us, anyway.

Could it be, though, that you find something more romantic where you hadn't looked for it before?

OUNDJIAN That's a different issue; there are things in Mozart that can be very romantic. In fact, I don't think there is any such thing as a "Romantic" composer. I mean, don't tell me that Mozart isn't romantic, or Beethoven.

HARADA Or Schubert.

OUNDJIAN These great artists—they were human beings, and if they expressed these wonderful, varied emotions, how could they not be romantic? On the other hand, there's the question of style, and to play Mozart with a big, wobbly vibrato and a big, thick sound. . . .

HARADA I think interpretation should change over the years. Somebody once mentioned to me an article by a European violinist who said that we didn't have the right feeling for Beethoven because we didn't experience World War II. Over there, they had a very hard life and she thought that without that you can't play Beethoven. I suspect she heard our very early records and it's true, our approach was quite different then. We didn't understand very much about the agony in his life. But we grow up, we get older, we go through all kinds of things—things that should come out in the way we make music. We feel differently about it now than we did ten or 15 years ago. I think we play better. Anything creative that you do, it's always evolving.

OUNDJIAN Yes, we've learned a lot about agony, and also about resignation, by playing Beethoven.

Isn't reading what people write about you rather a mistake?

Christian Steiner

Violinist Mikhail Kopelman, at left, joined the Tokyo and was quickly integrated.

OUNDJIAN Oh, we can accept these things; people have different opinions. But you're right. Charles Rosen said a very good thing: "Music criticism should be to musicians what ornithology is to birds." It has to exist, but we can't read it.

What about audiences? They have an impact on performances, don't they?

OUNDJIAN Definitely. The energy from an audience is quite astonishing, and there are so many kinds of silent audiences.

Do you find that your playing changes at all in response to the audiences, and their reactions to you?

OUNDJIAN A bit, at least. We can sense the need of an audience, and instinctively, even if we may not want to, we react. Let's say you're playing in a very small town for people who haven't had our kind of music in their blood for generations. You may want to give them just the music, but that doesn't seem to be enough, because Pink Floyd is down the road and they need to have it proved to them that it's OK to come and listen to Beethoven instead. There is the danger then of trying to give too much impact to things that could be rather subtle and beautiful just by themselves. You start to shout instead of speaking in a normal voice, and you speak instead of whispering, and everything can begin to change—the music can lose its breathing quality. It's not even a question of tempo, it's a question of letting the music breathe, have its time, have its space. That's one reason we want to avoid any kind of aggressive playing; we just don't enjoy it. And if we don't enjoy our own performance, how can the audience?

There is one more area I want to explore and I've saved it for last, because it's of very special interest to me. In your work with the young quartets you coach, what do you feel is most important for them to learn? How do you help four people to become a quartet?

IKEDA One big thing I feel they need to work on is the vibrato. Sometimes the two violinists will have a totally different approach, and

sometimes it's so big and fast you can't tell what intonation they are trying to play. Because the vibrato is one thing that you do maybe 95 per-
cent unconsciously, you can't just think about it and then try to do it; it
has to happen more or less like a habit. But if you have a bad habit, you
have to start from scratch. So it takes a lot of work to correct that, and
then it's not really coaching, it's almost like a private lesson.

What do you do with the other three in the meantime?
IKEDA They listen, and I think they learn from it, too.

HARADA It can be a very difficult situation. I don't want to feel I'm giving a lesson, especially to the violinists, so sometimes I ignore the technical problems. What I try to do is tell them how to start rehearsing,
how to make music. It's similar to what we try to do in our own
rehearsals. I tell them that it's very important to have the same pulse,
feel the same stride; you can start with that. Listen carefully to the cello;
does the vibrato have to be so fast right at the beginning? That sort of
thing. It takes a long time. Teaching anything is very difficult. It takes a
lot of patience and energy.

ISOMURA But it is very important for the students to study chamber
music.

OUNDJIAN That is perhaps the very most important thing for any
musician.

ISOMURA Especially the string-quartet literature. You learn how to
make very satisfying music with the least number of players. I also think
teaching is very good for me, because it forces me to think about what
I am doing.

   Another thing: Some students are just studying with us in order to
learn to play quartet or to study the literature, but there are some others who want to become a quartet, and I love to see that. Some want
to do it because they love playing quartet so much, and that makes
me happy, but others think that if they stick together for half a year or
so and play decently, they can make a career of it. And I know it's not
that easy. So when I coach groups who are ambitious in that way, I try
to be very strict and tell them how hard it is. It all depends on the students, what they are looking for, what I can do for them. It's hard to
generalize about what I teach them, but I always have a great time
teaching.

HARADA When I was studying, the teacher was very strict, and whatever he told us to do, we had to do it. I can't be like that. It's different
now from 15 or 20 years ago.

*I don't mind teachers who are demanding, but who is anybody to say, "It
should go like this"?*
OUNDJIAN That's right. What is a teacher supposed to do? Teach
people how to teach themselves, for the rest of their lives. If you tell

Recordings

Brahms: Quintet for Clarinet and Strings, Op. 115 in B Minor; Weber: Quintet for Clarinet and Strings, Op. 34, J. 182, in B-Flat. With Richard Stoltzman, clarinet (RCA 68033).

Beethoven: Quartet in C Minor, Op. 18, No. 4; Quartet in F Minor, Op. 95, "Serioso"; Quartet in F, Op. 135 (RCA 68038).

Beethoven: The Complete String Quartets (RCA 61621).

Beethoven: The Early String Quartets (Quartet in F, Op. 18, No. 1; Quartet in G, Op. 18, No. 2; Quartet in F [after Piano Sonata, Op. 14, No. 1]; Quartet in D, Op. 18, No. 3; Quartet in C Minor, Op. 18, No. 4; Quartet in B-Flat, Op. 8, No. 6; Quartet in A, Op. 18, No. 5; Quintet in C, Op. 29). With Pinchas Zukerman, viola (RCA 61284).

Beethoven: The Middle String Quartets (Quartet in F, Op. 59, No. 1, "Rasumovsky"; Quartet in E Minor, Op. 59, No. 2, "Rasumovsky"; Quartet in E-Flat, Op. 74, "Harp;" Quartet in C, Op. 59, No. 3 "Rasumovsky"; Quartet in F Minor, Op. 95, "Serioso" (RCA 60462).

Beethoven: The Late String Quartets (Quartet in E-Flat, Op. 127; Quartet in C-Sharp Minor, Op. 131; Quartet in B-Flat, Op. 130; Grosse Fuge, Op. 133; Quartet in A Minor, Op. 132; Quartet in F, Op. 135 (RCA 60975).

Boccherini: Quintet No. 6 in G, G. 450, and Quintet No. 4 in D, G. 448; Castelnuovo-Tedesco: Quintet, Op. 143. With Kazuhito Yamashita, guitar (RCA 60421).

Brahms: Quartet in C Minor, Op. 51, No. 1; Quartet in B-Flat, Op. 67, No. 3 (Vox Cum Laude 9012).

Debussy: Quartets; Ravel: Quartets (Sony Classical 35147).

Dvořák: Piano Quintet in A, Op. 81; String Quartet in F, Op. 96. With Hiroko Sakamura, piano (Sony Classical 44920).

Haydn: Quartet in D, Op. 20, No. 4; Quartet in F Minor, Op. 20, No. 5 (DG 2531 380).

Haydn: Quartet in G, Op. 76, No. 1; Brahms: Quartet in A Minor, Op. 51, No. 2 (DG 2555 005).

Haydn: Six String Quartets, Op. 50 (DG 2709 060).

Haydn: Quartets, Op. 76, "Erdody"; Quartet in G, Op. 76, No. 1; Quartet in D Minor, Op. 76, No. 2, "Fifths"; Quartet in C, Op. 76,

No. 3, "Emperor"; Quartet in B-Flat, Op. 76, No. 4, "Sunrise"; Quartet in D, Op. 76, No. 5; Quartet in E-Flat, Op. 76, No. 6 (Sony Classical 53522).

I Will Breathe a Mountain: Songs of Barber, Bernstein, and Bolcom. With Marilyn Horne, mezzo-soprano; Martin Katz, piano (RCA 68771).

Janáček and Bartók: Complete String Quartets. (RCA 68286).

Mozart: Clarinet Quintet in A, K. 581. With Richard Stoltzman, clarinet (RCA 60723).

Mozart: Flute Quartets in D, K. 285; in G, K. 285a; in C, K. 285b; in A, K. 298; and in F, K. 370. With James Galway, flute (RCA 60442).

Mozart: Four Complete Quartets for Flute and Strings. With Paula Robison, flute (Vanguard Classics 4001).

Mozart: String Quartet in C, K. 465; String Quartet in B-Flat, K. 589 (DG 2530 468).

Mozart: String Quintet in C, K. 515; String Quintet in G Minor, K. 516. With Pinchas Zukerman, viola (RCA 60940).

Ravel: Introduction and Allegro. With Nancy Allen, harp; Ransom Wilson, flute; David Schifrin, clarinet (Angel DS37339).

Ravel: Quartet in F, Introduction and Allegro; Debussy: Quartet, Op. 10, in G Minor. With James Galway, flute; Richard Stoltzman, clarinet; Heidi Lehwalder, harp (RCA 62552).

Respighi: Il Tramonto, Dieta Silvane, and Five Songs. With Renata Scotto, soprano (Vox Cum Laude 9039).

Schubert: Quartet in C Minor, D. 703; Quartet in D Minor, D. 810 (Vox Cum Laude 9001).

Schubert: Quartet No. 9 in G Minor, D. 173; Quartet No. 13 in A, D. 804 (RCA 7750).

Schubert: Quartet No. 14 in D Minor, D. 810, "Death and the Maiden"; Quartet No. 4 in C, D. 46 (RCA 7990).

Schubert: Quartet No. 15 in G (RCA 60199).

Schumann: Piano Quintet in E-Flat, Op. 44; Piano Concerto in A, Op. 54. With Alicia de Larrocha, piano (RCA 61279).

Takemitsu: A Way A Lone; Barber: Quartet, Op. 11; Britten: Quartet in C, No. 2, Op. 36 (RCA 61387).

them, "Do it like this," they haven't learned anything. To make them *think,* that's what I spend my time trying to do—make them see a point of view and give them a chance to think about it, even if they disagree with it.

So far we've talked only about the inexperienced groups, but sometimes we've also had very good ones. My first experience coaching was with a very young group who had all had chamber-music experience; in fact, all but one of them had played together before. They were already on a high level, matching bow strokes very well, and their intonation was good. Their problem was that they grossly exaggerated all

their pacing. They had been told, "You've got to make music, you've got to make things happen; look, it's exciting here, move forward; look, it's relaxed here . . ." and so on. It's good for kids to be told that, but in the end, one has to learn how to do these things without being so obvious about it. So I spent an entire hour and 15 minutes talking about pacing, about how to move from one tempo character to another without changing the tempo.

Then, in the last two years, we had the Franciscan Quartet studying with us, and that was a great pleasure, because they could do pretty much anything you asked of them. That kind of situation is very different; you can really learn from such students, and they can adjust so quickly to suggestions. And teaching a very gifted student is harder than teaching a very gifted quartet, because one person really needs your guidance and you are the only guide, but a quartet, when they are all gifted, they can basically teach one another.

Current quartet members (left to right) Mikhail Kopelman, Kikuei Ikeda, Kazuhide Isomura, and new cellist Clive Greensmith.

Christian Steiner

Can you show them how to do that?

OUNDJIAN We say, "When you're listening to each other, if you hear something you don't like, don't be shy, say it—but say it in a nice way." That's crucial. Everybody should learn diplomacy, whether it's in chamber music or politics or whatever.

Do you generally get your groups preformed, or do you put them together?

OUNDJIAN Some of each. This year, we tried to let them have a chance to choose each other, so that when they say, "I don't like him," we can say, "Well, you picked him, now you stick with it."

You mean they tend to fall apart?

OUNDJIAN Oh, yes.

Can you do anything to help prevent that?

OUNDJIAN Not if they fall apart because they are just so different that they really can't get along. But if they fall apart because there was a lack of caring about how they addressed each other, or because something went wrong and they didn't have the courage to confront the issue and clear the air, then you can say, "Well, if you could have been more mature about this, you could have saved the quartet." We had one case in a six-week summer course—this happened at the end of the fourth week— that was like a psychiatric ward for the four of us with the four of them. We all came to meet with them and talk with them, and they were so touched that they stayed together. It was amazing. They were embarrassed, and they thought, "We can't break up now, after all that; we have to make an effort," and it proved that they could work together.

It also proves that if the teachers care enough . . .

OUNDJIAN Exactly. I think that is the most important thing for a teacher, to make the students feel that you want to help them, you can help them, and they will improve. And then you can find something to believe in, something of value in any situation.

The Borodin
String Quartet

The Borodin String Quartet was founded in 1945 by fellow students from the Moscow Conservatory. At first they called themselves the Moscow Philharmonic Quartet, but in 1955 they changed their name to the Borodin. In those days the group was the up-and-coming representative of the younger generation, contrasting with the established and venerable Beethoven Quartet.

Since then the Borodin has made its reputation on its own terms—and been strongly affected by the political changes of its homeland. Its personnel changes have continued since this interview in late 1995: Mikhail Kopelman, former first violinist, now plays that role with the Tokyo String Quartet (see page 44); Ruben Aharonian has taken his place with the Borodin. The violist is now Igor Naidin. Violinist Andrei Abramenkov and founding member and cellist Valentin Berlinsky are still members of the group.

A Quartet Reborn

"When musicians perform a work, that is its second birth," says Valentin Berlinsky, the cellist of the Borodin String Quartet. "A work is born again every time it is performed."

This statement aptly describes the quartet's approach: the players seem indeed to recreate the music, becoming one with it and with one another. Their phrasing, dynamics, and articulation are totally unanimous, with hardly a look or gesture. Their sound is flawlessly pure, smooth as silk and warm as velvet, and so homogeneous that it seems to be spun from a single substance. They need no outward show, make no effort to project, to underline, to impress; we are drawn into their world and compelled to follow them. Mikhail Kopelman, the first violinist, is in particular a matchless virtuoso with a superb, effortless technique and a glorious tone. Their inwardness, concentration, and intensity are so riveting that it is easy to believe we are witnessing an act of creation, a second birth.

The theme of rebirth also has a special resonance for the Borodin Quartet's history. The group just celebrated the 50th anniversary of its founding in 1945 by four students of the Moscow Conservatory, including Berlinsky, the only original member still with the group, and violinist Rostislav Dubinsky, leader of the quartet until 1975. (Dubinsky emigrated to America, where he established himself as the founder of the Borodin Piano Trio and as a much-sought-after chamber-music coach. Much later he wrote a fascinating book about his years with the Borodin Quartet called *Stormy Applause* [Northeastern University Press, 1992], which describes, among other things, the political background against which the group's numerous personnel changes took place.) The present ensemble consists of Berlinsky, Dmitri Shebalin, who became its violist in the 1950s, and violinists Kopelman (who replaced Dubinsky) and Andrei Abramenkov, both of whom joined the group in the 1970s. Kopelman is much the youngest of the four; when he took over as first violinist, he was a year younger than the quartet, which had existed for 30 years. Berlinsky says with unconcealed pride, "Many skeptics believed that with Dubinsky's departure, the quartet would cease to exist, but we—the three remaining members—knew it would survive." Clearly, another rebirth.

The Borodin Quartet started coming to America in the 1960s with Dubinsky. The present group came in 1976 on its first trip abroad, and this was also the first time I heard it. The program notes of the concert stated that the two older members considered themselves "the keepers of the quartet's glorious tradition" and that the new members were expected to conform and adapt to it—not exactly the collaboration of equals that is my idea of a string quartet. The playing reflected this attitude: stunning in its perfection and control, it was cool and uninvolved; the players seemed to stand outside the music, too restrained and inhibited to let it move them.

On its most recent visit to New York, in 1994, the quartet presented the complete quartets of Shostakovich, with which it has been closely associated ever since the original members worked on them with the composer himself. Though this does indeed create a strong link with tradition, the reference to conformity had vanished from the program. The playing, too, while as spectacular as ever technically and tonally, had lost its constraint and detachment and acquired a new depth and freedom. The players entered into the world of Shostakovich's music with complete identification and made it their own; the authority and authenticity of their interpretation brought out its strengths and concealed its weaknesses. They played the 15 quartets in approximately chronological order in five concerts, and while such a total immersion may not be the best way to listen to this pervasively bleak, emotionally devastating music, the performances made the series one of the season's highlights. The playing grew progressively more involved and expressive, and the cumulative impact of the cycle was overwhelming. For the final quartet, the stage lights were turned off and candles were lit on the music stands, creating a solemn, devotional atmosphere. As Berlinsky explains, "For the Borodin Quartet, the 15th Quartet is the requiem Shostakovich wrote for himself."

How did this group emerge from countless political and personal upheavals not only unscathed, but as an incomparable string quartet, with a distinctive style and personality? How did it achieve such integration and homogeneity?

Asking for an interview required all my courage: approaching them as a total stranger, I was as intimidated by their lofty status and playing style as by the language barrier. I visited them backstage halfway through the cycle and appealed to Kopelman, who speaks very creditable English, having emigrated to America and lived in Brooklyn since 1993. He was warm and friendly, and after consulting his colleagues he told me they were willing to talk, but only through an interpreter (although two of them know German, my own native language). They themselves will provide a translator who is knowledgeable about music and quartet playing. A daunting prospect, but, despite my misgivings, the opportunity of a personal meeting with these wonderful players was too tempting to miss.

Left to right, Mikhail Kopelman, Andrei Abramenkov, Dmitri Shebalin, and Valentin Berlinsky.

I find them in a smoke-filled hotel room where they had been rehearsing—apparently warnings of the dangers of smoking have not penetrated what used to be the Iron Curtain. Vestiges of the Old Order are also clearly perceptible in the players' initially distant, formal behavior, which, however, gradually relaxes. The interpreter is a young Russian violinist, Emil Chudnovsky, whose mother, the noted violinist Nina Beilina, brought him to America when he was six and taught him to play the violin as well as to remember his native tongue. He does a fine job of not only translating but also mediating between two parties, who speak different languages in more senses than one.

The interview is fascinating, but also unsettling and frustrating. The presence of a translator places an invisible barrier between my hosts and me, eliminating any sense of direct, immediate contact. My questions evoke long, lively discussions among the players, punctuated by laughter I cannot share. I watch in helpless envy as Chudnovsky avidly follows these consultations and then relays the result: usually a brief conclusion or summary. Their answers are at times quite unrelated to my questions, more like a replaying of some predetermined response than a spontaneous reaction. Is this due to misunderstanding, miscommunication, or ingrained, automatic caution? Questions on specific technical

What they play

The members of the Borodin String Quartet all use first-class Italian instruments, but they are not their own. They are on loan to them from the Russian State Collection as long as they play in the quartet. At the time of this interview, Kopelman's violin was an Antonio Stradivari of 1710, loaned to him six years after he joined the group, and Abramenkov's violin a J.B. Guadagnini of 1735. Shebalin played a Lorenzo Storioni viola for 25 years, and Berlinsky's cello was a Carlo Bergonzi.

Jonathan Weaver

and musical matters prove difficult to explain and seem unwelcome. The players are pleased when I say I have heard them on several previous occasions, but trying to express my admiration adequately through an intermediary is hopelessly frustrating.

Berlinsky, the oldest as well as the most senior member of the quartet, seems to be the semiofficial spokesman. He is serious and a bit solemn but soon becomes very warm and animated. Kopelman, whose encouraging nods and smiles show that he understands my questions, eventually becomes impatient with the cumbersome process of translation and simply begins to answer me in English. The other two appear a bit distant and uninvolved, though not without humor in conversation within the group.

The musicians are surprisingly willing to talk about the political changes in Russia and freely admit that "life is very difficult and the economy is in a terrible state." Shebalin, who had taught at the Moscow Conservatory for 25 years, left in 1992, as have a great many other teachers. "The salary of a professor is miserly, so obviously, if one receives a handsome offer abroad, he will accept it. Some teachers are contracted to work in various other conservatories abroad; some have emigrated entirely, though they are often still Russian residents."

I ask whether people are emigrating because life is now more difficult than previously. Berlinsky answers, "It's not exactly fair to say that life is now more difficult, but it is fair to say that it is a lot easier to leave."

What effect is the new government having on the lives and careers of Russian musicians?

"A positive effect," Berlinsky responds. "Formerly, everything was controlled by ideology. Today, there is no longer any centralization. Goskonzert, the former centralized state-owned managerial agency, is now Gos Corporation, a public shareholder company that works along Western lines, like a company on the stock exchange. The shareholders include the Borodin Quartet, [pianist] Sviatoslav Richter, [cellist] Natalia Guzman, the Bolshoi Theater, and the Board of Aviation." "The Board of Aviation?" I ask in surprise. "Well," they explain, "it contributes money."

The quartet's general manager is in England, but the players continue to work with the Moscow Philharmonic and to be in residence at the Conservatory. I ask whether the artists can choose where they will and will not play concerts.

"Yes, today the artists are their own bosses; the corporation only takes care of such mundane matters as tickets, visas, etc.," Chudnovsky translates for them all. "But the main thing is that formerly, you would have to play in just about every little place with a stop sign, even those too small to have a concert hall. Now the circuit has become a lot narrower. You go to the major cities instead of traveling around for months at a time, going nowhere."

Kopelman adds, "Today, the greatest problem is transportation. There are no flights, there is no gas. For example, it takes about 40 hours to get from Moscow to the western border of the Ukraine. It used to take two and a half hours by plane, but now there are no planes, though there are the beginnings of some connections. When I could not get to the Ukraine last year, I was told, 'Well, you weren't lucky.' Can you imagine anyone saying that in America?"

The quartet also plays abroad more than before, and that is of course more rewarding financially. From 1990 to 1992, it was in residence at the Aldeburgh Festival in England, where the players coached ensembles and held master classes.

Steering the conversation to musical subjects, I ask Kopelman what it was like to become part of a quartet that had been together for 30 years. "It is of course incredibly difficult," he answers, "and requires a great deal of time and work. I came to it unprepared, without a repertoire, never having played in a professional quartet. I had to begin from scratch, to learn from my colleagues, to rethink many of the things I had been doing on the violin: intonation, vibrato, bow distribution, everything related to ensemble playing as opposed to solo or orchestra playing."

Shebalin adds, "It was a mutual growing together, because if Misha had to adapt himself to the quartet, the quartet also had to adapt itself to him."

I ask how they had found him. They tell me in some surprise that they knew his address; then, laughing at the misunderstanding, Berlinsky explains, "We had received some recommendations from friends and fellow professors; there were several candidates, some quite famous—no names need be mentioned. We initially met Misha in the buffet of the Moscow Philharmonic. At the first rehearsal soon afterward, we began by playing Haydn quartets—some which the group had never played or performed. We were all sight-reading so everybody would have the same handicap. And of course there are certain Haydn quartets where God help all those who attempt to play them! Because Misha's sight-reading was phenomenal and his tone complemented ours, and because we got along easily from a personal point of view, we decided to look no further."

Finding a second violinist was quite a long, difficult process, Chudnovsky explains, but once found, "Abramenkov integrated into the quartet without any difficulties, without growing pains." He had worked in Rudolf Barshai's chamber orchestra for 16 years, which was a great school for chamber-music playing, in part because the members formed quartets among themselves. The only problem was the repertoire. For four months, the quartet rehearsed six to eight hours a day, at least. They even left town, went to the suburbs, where there was no phone, no television, and worked for the coming season. In this way, they acquired a fairly extensive repertoire—in fact, six different programs. A number of programs had already been set before Dubinsky left, even given to foreign managements who plan several seasons ahead, but not a single concert was canceled as a result of the personnel changes.

The current ensemble played its first concert in 1976, in a city that was formerly called Gorky, now Nijniy Novgorod. "It is a city with which the quartet is very tightly interwoven," says Chudnovsky, "and forms an interesting symbolic link in their career. It was there they played the last concert with Dubinsky and the first one with the new second violinist. In other words, the trial city. It is a musical Mecca; my mother taught there, its Philharmonic is magnificent."

I am eager to talk about Shostakovich and his quartets, asking what it had been like to work with him on his music. With a faraway expression, Berlinsky says, "Several precious reliquaries have remained: some letters from him to the quartet, one written after we made him a gift of an album of our recording of the 11 quartets that had been written at the time. It contains a detailed analysis of the performance." Hoping to bring him back to earth, I ask whether the composer had helped them while they were preparing the quartets. "Every quartet was played for him before it was performed publicly, but of course it's one thing to perform something in public and something else entirely to record it. The letter said more or less that he gets great pleasure from listening to the recording and is very grateful for the work it represents."

Current members, left to right: Igor Naidin, Valentin Berlinsky, Andrei Abramenkov, and Ruben Aharonian.

Did Shostakovich come to their rehearsals to offer suggestions? "When we had worked out a quartet for ourselves and were ready for his comments, we would play it for him," Berlinsky says. "All his quartets except the first and the last were premiered by the Beethoven Quartet [an older, highly respected Russian quartet]." The Borodin members will not say whether they themselves ever got any advice from Shostakovich. Berlinsky only remarks, "He was one of the very few composers who know precisely what they want, and he was absolutely scrupulous about writing it into the parts. If something like tempo or dynamics did not sound exactly as he imagined, he would be able to say so right away."

I ask if they follow his often very uncomfortable bowing indications. Kopelman says, in English, "I don't." Berlinsky adds, "These markings are a means to realizing the expression the composer seeks; one performer may do it in one way, another performer in another way."

We talk about the late Shostakovich quartets and about the 15th being a requiem. I say I thought the 13th was also, in a way, a requiem. "It's more about pain and loss," Berlinsky answers, "It's not exactly sane music . . . it's very uncertain, very uneasy, something like delirium,

Recordings

Beethoven: Grosse Fuge Quartet; Shostakovich: Elegy String Quartet, String Quartet No. 8 (Russian Disc RDCD 11087).

Beethoven: Quartet No. 11, "Quartetto serioso"; Haydn: Quartets, Op. 64; Schoenberg: Quartet No. 2. With L. Belobragina, soprano (MK MKA 418019).

Borodin: Quartets Nos. 1 and 2 (EMI Classics CDC 47795).

Brahms: Quartets Nos. 1 and 3 (Teldec 90889).

Brahms: Quartet No. 2; Piano Quintet. With Elizo Virzaladze, piano (Teldec 97461).

Haydn: The Seven Last Words of Christ (Teldec 92373).

Mahler: Piano Quartet; Schnittke: String Quartet No. 3; Piano Quintet. With L. Berlinsky, piano (Virgin Classics 59040).

Medtner: Piano Quintet. With E. Evetlanov, piano (Russian Disc 11019).

Russian Miniatures (Teldec 94572).

Schubert: Quartet No. 10; String Quartet No. 12, "Quartettsatz"; Quartet No. 13, "Rosamunde" (Virgin Classics 59047).

Schubert: String Quintet, D. 956. With Misha Milman, cello (Teldec 94564).

Shostakovich: String Octet, the complete String Quintets. With the Prokofiev String Quartet; Sviatoslav Richer, piano (Melodiya 6-74321-40711).

Shostakovich: Quartets No. 2 and 12 (Virgin Classics 59281).

Shostakovich: Quartet Nos. 3, 7, and 8 (Virgin Classics 59041).

Shostakovich: Quartet No. 12; Piano Quintet. With Sviatoslav Richter, piano (Intaglio ING 7561).

Stenhammar: Quartet No. 3; Sentimental Romances. With B. Lysell, violin (Swedish Society SCD 1032).

Tchaikovsky: Quartets Nos. 1–3; Souvenir de Florence (EMI Classics 49775 and Teldec 90422).

which is not typical of a requiem." It ends on a long, high, unison note for the three upper strings, that stops abruptly at the peak of a tremendous crescendo; it has been compared to a blinding white light, and then—there's nothing. At the Borodin Quartet's last concert in the Shostakovich series, Berlinsky joined that note gradually, making the effect even more blinding.

How do these musicians rehearse, with one living in Brooklyn and three in Russia, I wonder aloud. "It's harder to rehearse between Brooklyn and Manhattan than between Brooklyn and Moscow," says Kopelman, laughing. "But we tour and perform all the time. Now we'll be in Moscow for almost two months; there will be a big concert tour for the 50th anniversary."

The group's repertoire encompasses the literature from Haydn to Bartók and includes both romantic and contemporary Russian composers. They recorded the Shostakovich quartets years ago for EMI and now have a contract with Teldec Classics International. My special favorites among their recordings are the quartets and the *Souvenir de Florence* by Tchaikovsky, played with captivating charm and wit, the dance movements a swirl of riotous color; Haydn's *Seven Last Words*, which they conceive as a more religious, dramatic experience than most European and American groups, and a wonderfully austere but romantic performance of the quartets and piano quintet by Brahms. All are distinguished by an intoxicatingly beautiful sound with every line standing out, great expressiveness, eloquent rhetoric and poetry, and pacing that is both spacious and flowing.

The Manhattan
String Quartet

One of America's leading chamber ensembles, the Manhattan String Quartet has been playing throughout the U.S. and Europe for nearly three decades. The current members are Eric Lewis and Calvin Wiersma, first and second violinists; John Dexter, viola; and Chris Finckel, cello. When they were interviewed in 1991 for the following article, with a somewhat different membership, they had just become the first American group to bring the Shostakovich quartets to Russia.

Musical Ambassadors

The Manhattan String Quartet, as its name implies, was formed at the Manhattan School of Music in New York, where first violinist Eric Lewis and cellist Judith Glyde (later husband and wife) met as students in the late 1960s. They played a lot of chamber music and were coached by violist Lillian Fuchs and violinist Rachmael Weinstock; the latter, having been the leader of the old Manhattan Quartet in the '30s, decided that it should have a modern incarnation and asked Lewis to form a new Manhattan Quartet.

The group played its first concert in 1970, went on to study with the Lenox Quartet in Binghamton, and then got its first job as quartet in residence at Grinnell College in Iowa. But the Lewises missed the East Coast so much that they returned to New York in 1975, and at that time also changed partners: Eric's brother Roy came in as second violinist and Judith's sister Rosemary as violist. This would seem to make them one of the most family-oriented quartets in history. Judith Glyde says she found it very natural, having played with her family all her life ("though playing with your husband does present different complications"), while violist John Dexter, who joined them in 1980, says that playing with so much family not his own feels fine.

In 1989 at New York's Town Hall, the quartet gave a five-concert series called "The Soul of Dmitri Shostakovich," presenting his 15 string quartets as well as the Piano Quintet, after having taken several trips to the Soviet Union in connection with the project. During that time, they recorded some of these works for Centaur Records, and they have just released the complete cycle on a new six-volume set of CDs for ESS.A.Y. Recordings. In 1990, they performed the complete string quartets of Bartók and Schoenberg in four concerts at Town Hall, so our conversation revolved around the different problems and rewards of a total immersion in the works of these three composers.

What gave you the idea of playing all this Shostakovich?
ROY LEWIS We started with No. 8. It's the one everybody starts with, because it's a wonderful piece. People really respond to it emotionally and you can easily put it on any program. But we were intrigued, because we heard he wrote 14 more quartets, and when we asked around for another good one, some friends suggested No. 3. We found very much the same kind of audience response, and it was also really exciting and meaningful for us to play. Next, we tried No. 10 and it was *wonderful,* and we said, "Why is nobody playing these pieces?"

Many of these quartets seem so autobiographical, full of personal coding, almost.
ERIC LEWIS Yes, that's what we're doing, decoding, as we live with these pieces over the years and meet other people who have played them, particularly people from the Soviet Union who knew Shostakovich. It is a fascinating picture, and a big part of it came into focus for us last summer when we got together with [Rostislav] Dubinsky, the former leader of the Borodin Quartet, and now the violinist of the Borodin Trio. We were in Canada at a festival and he came up for a week to teach and talk about Shostakovich.

DEXTER We knew that he was a great violinist and a fine musician and coach, and we wanted to meet him and play for him as much as we could. And what he told us about No. 8 was fascinating, because it's obviously encoded with all sorts of biographical ideas, but what they refer to was not really clear to us. Of course, that happens in many of the quartets, especially after No. 8, but this seems to be the focal one. Dubinsky, who knew Shostakovich and obviously knew a lot more about Russian music in general than we did, could point out passages with an inner meaning in that particular quartet—for example, the use of the motive that spells Shostakovich's initials, in the German note names: D-E♭-C-B [E♭ is S in German, and B is H].

There's also a passage toward the end of the fourth movement where the cello suddenly has this very ethereal melody at the top of the range, while the rest of us are just holding notes and commenting generally on what she is saying. When we were learning the piece, this seemed like a special moment, but we didn't know what it meant. Then Dubinsky told us that this melody is a quote from Shostakovich's opera, *Lady Macbeth of Mtsensk,* where it is the motif for the emotional high point of the whole opera: the heroine, Katerina, has just married a man who is completely unfaithful, a real cad, a jerk, the worst possible word you can use in print. She committed murder because she loves him and thinks he loves her; she degraded herself to the utmost, and what she's saying to this melody is, "At last! The whole day I did not see you; the pain, the weariness and sorrow, all is forgotten once you are with me, Sergei, Sergei. . . ." And then, right after exposing herself emotionally like that, she discovers that he's taken up with another woman. It's a complete disaster for her, and she grabs the other girl and pushes her into a deep lake and jumps in after her.

A later incarnation: left to right, Eric Lewis, Roy Lewis, Chris Finckel, and John Dexter.

But why did he put the melody into this particular quartet?

ROY LEWIS Because he had been a Communist, he believed in the revolution, he debased himself for it, and then he felt betrayed by what happened. That's my own interpretation, because just before that moment in the quartet, he uses a song in the two violins, an old Russian tune about suffering and languishing in prison.

ERIC LEWIS If you put that together with the dedication of this quartet, "To the victims of war and fascism," you can see the connection. And then, Dubinsky told us a very important story about the premiere of the piece at the Union of Composers.

DEXTER The official line was that it was dedicated to the victims of war and fascism in Russia, the people who fought in the war against the Nazis. So after the premiere, some official stood up and went on and on about what a wonderful piece it was, and how it glorified the Russian sacrifice and the Soviet struggle and the victory of the proletariat, and Shostakovich stood up. "I protest," he said, "that is not true; this is my personal statement against *all* sorts of fascism," and sat down.

And what happened?

ERIC LEWIS Everybody realized that though he was a very quiet, introverted person, he was obviously referring to the repression in his own country, and they were totally stunned that he'd put his life in danger like that.

DEXTER The amazing thing is that nothing happened; it did not appear in the papers, there was no record of it in print. Dubinsky made a point of that.

ROY LEWIS I remember my trepidation when we first played the Eighth Quartet in the Soviet Union, in 1985. But the reception was astounding; people were quite vociferous. They were so thankful that we were playing this music that had such great meaning for them.

ERIC LEWIS A critic heard it, one who had written about that famous premiere. He told us that at the first hearing, he had thought it was a light, sort of coquettish piece. And then when we played it, it was a revelation to him, because Russian performers playing that kind of emotional music are self-conscious about exposing their feelings, especially in a climate where they are worried about showing their vulnerability. But we were coming from another place, and he said, "It's amazing that this revelation came to us through an American group, so that we could see ourselves mirrored."

When we first learned No. 8, we went through the whole quartet and put all sorts of associations with these important themes, and the one association Judy came up with for her solo was a scene in a movie we saw about the Holocaust. It's set in Romania, in a place where there is this gigantic field full of daffodils. And they show this place and then they tell you that the reason it's so fertile is that the soil is five feet deep of human remains, because it's outside one of those crematoriums.

GLYDE It was a scene of great calm and peacefulness, and great beauty—

ERIC LEWIS —incredible beauty, but incredible horror at the same time, and that's the way she played that theme. And it used to almost destroy me every time I heard it, because of that image.

GLYDE But it's basically the same idea, the same emotion, as in the opera; the woman has great joy, she has great peace, and then she has great horror.

Did the opera ever get performed in Russia?

DEXTER Yes, it played to great acclaim at first, and then Stalin saw it and that was the end of it.

ERIC LEWIS That was really the first big trouble for Shostakovich, and that's another reason why that melody would be in that quartet: there were two periods when they clamped down on him, one in the '30s and one in the '40s, and the works from around both those periods are quoted in the quartets.

GLYDE At certain times of his life, he actually couldn't present them publicly at all.

ERIC LEWIS The Fourth Quartet is a good example of that. It was premiered in 1954, instead of in the late '40s, when it was written, because he felt that Stalin would probably give him trouble with all its obviously Jewish themes.

DEXTER Jewish-like.

ERIC LEWIS Yes, that's an important distinction. He didn't take Jewish folk songs, but he used the style. It was his way of protesting Soviet anti-Semitism.

I've noticed that many of the quartets are dedicated to a specific player.

ERIC LEWIS The late ones, to the players of the Beethoven Quartet. They were the ones who did the famous premiere of the Eighth, in 1960.

DEXTER The Beethoven was the established old quartet, and the Borodin was the new, excellent, up-and-coming quartet.

ERIC LEWIS They had a lively competition going on.

GLYDE I think perhaps Shostakovich felt that he had to make these dedications to the Beethoven Quartet, but then under cover he would slip a copy to the Borodin.

ROY LEWIS No. 11 is dedicated to the second violinist. After the piece was written, he died, and No. 12 has no second violin part for 40 bars. Then the second violin joins in; that's supposed to mean they have a new player. It's nice for me, because I don't have to be on time to rehearsals.

ERIC LEWIS I suppose, although it starts with death, that No. 12 is a reaffirmation of life.

What about No. 13, with the big viola part? It's dedicated to the violist, but he wasn't the one who played it.

ERIC LEWIS He was sick, and it was premiered by another guy. It's death, the whole piece—for me, anyway. Look at the end, this high B-flat, all three voices playing the same note, and look at this marking [a crescendo from *pp* to *sffff*]. For me, it's like this white light, and you're going toward death—and then it stops, just like that, and it's over.

GLYDE It's the first death piece, really.

DEXTER It foreshadows the last quartet in its spare writing.

ROY LEWIS Yes, the 15th. We were told a story about that in the Soviet Union by our interpreter, who was present when the piece was first played privately for Shotakovich. She said that by the end he was weeping openly, "because it's so much about death, and it is his own death."

He was sick by that time, wasn't he?

ROY LEWIS Yes, and you can really feel that this is something quite remarkable, you can tell from the tempo markings: Adagio, Adagio, Adagio molto, Molto adagio.

ERIC LEWIS It contains some of his most beautiful music; elegiac is the word for it.

We seem to have left out No. 14. . . . I'm glad you're laughing, but what's so funny in the midst of all this gloom?

What they play

Violinist Eric Lewis plays a J.B. Ceruti made in 1793. He has two bows, by Voirin and Nicolas Maire, and plays on Dominant strings with a thick E string by Hill. Roy Lewis plays a Guadagnini Brothers violin made in 1879. His bow is an H.R. Pfretzschner and he uses Dominant strings (the D is silver) with a Jargar E. Current second violinist Calvin Wiersma (second from left) plays an Honoré Derazey violin with a Fétique bow, and he uses Dominant strings with a Wondertone Gold Label E. Violist John Dexter has a Georges Chanot viola made in Paris in about 1840. He has three bows, by Simon, Eugene Sartory, and Tubbs, and plays on Dominant strings with a Jargar medium A string. Cellist Judith Glyde's instrument was made in 1964 by Max Frierz in New York City, and she uses a Vigneron bow. Chris Finckel (pictured below), the cellist now with the group, plays an anonymous 18th-century instrument with a Eugene Sartory bow, a Jargar A string, and Spirocore D, G, and C strings.

Christian Steiner

GLYDE Well, this quartet is dedicated to [Sergei] Shirinski, the cellist of the Beethoven Quartet. It was always very difficult to get a handle on how to play that little opening motive; I tried really hard to make something intelligent and musical out of it, but it always sounded to me like a very dumb tune.

ERIC LEWIS We played this piece on our last Russian tour in 1989 at the Union of Composers, and we asked Berlinsky, the cellist of the Borodin Quartet [see page 58], who has become friendly with us from our tours, "Tell us, what is going on in this piece, especially the first movement?" So—and let me remind you that this is the cellist of the Borodin talking about the cellist of the Beethoven String Quartet— Berlinsky said it was very well known all over Russia that Shirinski was a very shallow man, and the music is supposed to be played without intelligence!

GLYDE Someone actually used the words "kind of dumb." So I stopped worrying about it.

But the first violin gets this tune very soon afterwards; do you play it "dumb," too?

ERIC LEWIS No, you see, the cello has a falling line, but three bars later, I have a rising line, so I'm trying to raise it up into the higher realm of understanding [*laughter*].

Shostakovich, you know, conceived of his string quartets in one big arch. He wanted to write 24—he planned to go through all the keys, but he didn't make it. Also, the imprint of a quartet mentality through Beethoven and Bartók was very strong—the whole idea of cyclical metamorphosis and infinite variation that you find in the late Beethoven Quartets. There's stuff in the Second and Third Quartets that is reworked and comes back over and over and over again; it just seems to open up forever.

He started writing quartets in the middle of his life, so they are part of a mature period. It seems that he really needed the outlet of the string quartet to handle some of the internal, psychological pressures he was under. And to us, these pieces seem to be chapters in a continuous story, maybe especially because we played them all in one day.

How can that be done?

ERIC LEWIS I don't know how we did it. We started at 10 A.M. and ended at 10 P.M.

GLYDE We did it at Western Connecticut State University, a location where it might have some educational value to the community, and also because we hoped that not too many people would find out about it through the press. We didn't know if we'd make it to the end, just constantly playing for 12 hours.

ROY LEWIS We stopped for lunch and supper.

GLYDE It was an experiment, and it was great! It gave us a wonderful opportunity to take a look at the quartets from beginning to end in a continuous progression.

But it's not just the physical endurance, it's the emotional concentration!

ERIC LEWIS Yes, that was basically the challenge; it was like reading a Russian novel.

GLYDE Some people stayed the whole time. From my own point of view, there was only one problem: after playing for ten or 11 hours, you come to No. 15, where everything is very slow, but passion-filled, and at the very end, there is a gigantic cadenza, first for the cello and then for the violin, an explosion of activity. By that time, my fingers were so numb they barely made it. But there's a feeling, a style, that carries over from one quartet to the other. We found the more Shostakovich we played, the easier it was, techically and emotionally.

ROY LEWIS We developed our own interpretation.

DEXTER We simply jumped in and learned them; nobody else was playing them.

ERIC LEWIS But musicians in the Soviet Union play them. There is a quartet for each republic, and every one of them plays all the Shostakovich quartets.

GLYDE We had as many of them as possible listen to us, to get their impressions and learn from them.

Having just done the Schoenberg and Bartók quartets, how would you describe the difference between performing those and the Shostakovich?

DEXTER Well, for one thing, the Shostakovich are much easier to deal with; they aren't so demanding technically.

ROY LEWIS They have a transparency which is very difficult, and the ensemble is hard to achieve, but one of the reasons we're so committed to them is that they are players' pieces; you spend most of your time working on large emotional and interpretational issues, and that's why they give you so much enjoyment and satisfaction.

ERIC LEWIS To play them, a quartet has to develop a style and create a process of communicating, because there is so much that he did not write into the scores. So then it comes out sounding completely different from the quartet next door, and apparently that was his plan. He would listen to string quartets play his work and wouldn't say a word. They would ask, "Maestro, what shall we do here?" And he'd say, "I trust you to do what you want."

GLYDE While with Bartók, everything is so carefully written down— the tempo, the dynamics, the markings, the accents—that if you observe exactly what's in the score, including the metronome marks, it'll sound like Bartók.

ERIC LEWIS Schoenberg also gives you metronome markings at the beginning of the page, but in his instructions he says very explicitly, "Do not take these metronome markings literally!" Bartók was more of a performer, and I think he had a closer idea of how a tempo should work.

But Schoenberg, now, that's really hard, very dense, very difficult to hear. In the Third Quartet, nobody ever plays together—I think there's not one unison in the whole piece. In the Fourth Quartet, at least there are some rhythmic unisons, so even though we may not be playing the kind of tonalities that we understand, there is something to hang on to. Unlike Shostakovich, who really wrote for an audience, I think Schoenberg, at some point, got turned off by the audience—they were throwing so many arrows at him after the Second Quartet—and he decided to experiment and write for his own circle. The Third Quartet is the apex of that, and then he starts to move toward the audience again. There is great music in Schoenberg, even in the early quartet, with all that Brahms and Dvořák going on. You have to realize that his writing is still within the tradition of the Viennese School; there are a lot of gestures, rhythmic gestures, for example, that are very conservative.

ROY LEWIS Yes, the gesture of the music, that was paramount in his mind: the sigh in the falling line, the hope in the rising line, the valse tempo; he just imposed a new kind of personal, completely horizontal harmonic device on that structure.

Christian Steiner

Clockwise from upper left, Roy Lewis, Eric Lewis, Judith Glyde, and John Dexter.

ERIC LEWIS You know, as human beings, we have pulsation going on, and in music, in terms of the tones and combinations, that is consonance and dissonance, right? Now with the late Schoenberg quartets, you get *rid* of consonance entirely, but there's still harmonic pulsation, only it's in a dissonant universe. And for me, this is a reflection of the dissonant universe of the middle of the 20th century, which was a great horror to him—he was totally horrified, for example, by what was going on in Hitler's Germany, so what comes out in the music is a reflection of a neurotic, psychotic view of life.

DEXTER I don't believe that he sat down and figured out what was going to happen harmonically when he wrote the lines.

ERIC LEWIS I feel there are gradations of dissonance, but he was great enough to know when he went to a really heavy dissonance—whereas some of his disciples who use his system cannot make that distinction, because they're not as fully grounded in the post-Romantic idea. Anyone who could write post-Romantic piece like *Verklärte Nacht* is a great composer, a great musical mind.

Recordings

Adagio for Strings: *Dvořák Quartet, Op. 96; pieces by Wolf, Puccini, Turina, Gershwin, Kern, Barber (Newport Classic 60033).*

Beethoven: Quartet, Op. 59, No. 2; Mozart: Quartet, K.499 (MQ 1001).

Boatwright: Quartet No. 2 (Composers Recordings LP).

Chamber Music for Flute and Strings: *Works by Bergsma, Tovey, Villa Lobos, Beach. With Doriot Anthony Dwyer, flute (Koch 3-7001).*

Collins: String Quartet (Composers Recordings 644).

Music of Portugal: *Carneyro: String Quartet in D Minor; Peixinho: Episodios; Pires: Quartet (Educo LP).*

Parker: Songs for Eve, Echoes from the Hills (MHS 827161M).

Schubert: Quartet No. 14 (Centaur Records 2013).

Schubert: Quartet No. 15 in G Major, Op. 161 (Centaur Records 2023).

Shostakovich: Quartets Nos. 1, Op. 49; 2, Op. 68; and 3, Op. 73 (ESS.A.Y. 1007).

Shostakovich: Quartets Nos. 4, Op. 83; and 5, Op. 92 (ESS.A.Y. 1008).

Shostakovich: Quartets Nos. 6, Op. 101; 7, Op. 108; and 8, Op. 118 (ESS.A.Y. 1009).

Shostakovich: Quartets Nos. 9, Op. 117; and 10, Op. 118 (ESS.A.Y. 1010).

Shostakovich: Quartets Nos. 11, Op. 122; 12, Op. 133; and 13, Op. 138 (ESS.A.Y. 1012).

Shostakovich: Quartets Nos. 14, Op. 142; 15, Op. 144 (ESS.A.Y. 1013).

Two Oboe Quintets: *Bax, Bliss. With Bert Lucarelli, oboe (MHS LP).*

Two Quintets for Flute and Strings: *Molique, Romberg. With John Wion, flute (MHS LP 3402).*

Von Weber: Quintet for Clarinet and Strings; Introduction, Theme and Variations. With John Manasse, clarinet; Samuel Sanders, piano (XLNT Recordings 18004).

But how does one make him accessible to an audience?

ERIC LEWIS This was our problem: How to put character and all the other artistic things we are used to doing into something that is just so difficult to play.

DEXTER And to listen to.

I'm glad you feel that, too, although you know these pieces so well. I always think I'm dumb because I can't hear this music.

ROY LEWIS Well, I'd like to say, I get riled when I hear people say "it makes me feel dumb." I think if you hear a piece and don't like it, your reaction is perfectly valid. It bothers me especially when critics start writing so as to make the audience feel stupid, as can easily happen if people went to a concert and enjoyed the music, and then they read a review that says, "That was garbage," or "You know nothing, what you didn't like was wonderful." [*Laughter.*]

I feel dumb not when I don't like a piece, but when I don't know how to hear it.

ROY LEWIS Let's be frank, I wonder if you *can* listen to those late Schoenberg quartets. I think you can have a wonderful time looking at them, but really, I find it very hard myself to listen to them.

But then how can you play them?

ROY LEWIS Oh, it's fun to play them! Your brain starts jumping around, counting and thinking like mad. It's like cranking up a computer, when it starts crunching numbers at an incredibly high rate. You feel you're on the edge and it's very exciting. But to comprehend Schoenberg, you have to be able to separate the lines in each of the four instruments and assign them their particular structure: retrograde, inverted, or plain, and then to see those different variations superimposed one upon the other. That's how you have to listen to it and appreciate it.

And you can hear that?

ROY LEWIS Personally, I can't.

Well, I must say I find that very comforting. How do you rehearse this kind of thing?

ERIC LEWIS Bar by bar, and then put it together.

GLYDE Well, some of it. There's a lot that you can play as a whole; when you're physically in the music, it becomes much more interesting to ferret it out. We always try to get the larger sections first and then take it apart.

ROY LEWIS It's like any kind of an art; you have to learn to decide what you want to say with a piece, what is important, what your interpretation is. If it works logically in the end, you're happy, and if it doesn't, you try a different way.

ERIC LEWIS In other words, we still handle it in the classical ways of all music.

GLYDE But to go back to your earlier question: I think even in the best possible performance, not many people could really listen to Schoenberg and understand him; there would not be an immediate emotional response.

As there is with Shostakovich.

Roy Lewis

ERIC LEWIS That's the great surprise: the audience comes in expecting [Shostakovich's] quartets to be the usual contemporary experience, where we don't understand what's going on but it's good for us. And almost from the first note, they sit bolt upright. I think these are some of the most important quartets ever written.

Tell me about your trips to the USSR.

ROY LEWIS In 1985, we were invited to play Shostakovich quartets at the consulate in Leningrad and at the ambassador's residence in Moscow.

The quartet in Leningrad (St. Petersburg) during their 1986 tour of the Soviet Union.

GLYDE It was the week before the first summit meeting between [USSR President Mikhail] Gorbachev and [U.S. President Ronald] Reagan and the cultural-exchange conference in Geneva.

ROY LEWIS We were staying in the residence while they were negotiating, and we'd hear the daily progress reports and the ambassador's briefings. That was an extremely exciting time.

GLYDE It was a wonderful trip; I had a smile on my face for a week, my heart was so full of joy all the time.

ERIC LEWIS There was the first year of *glasnost* and the people were so excited; the atmosphere of hope was just amazing.

ROY LEWIS One of my peak memories from that trip is of a reception the night before we left, when a Soviet official from the Department of Culture came to me and said that a cultural-exchange agreement would be signed, and that they wanted us to come back as the first American group. We went back the next year, in 1986.

Had these quartets ever been played there by an American group?

ERIC LEWIS The only American quartet that we know had been there was the Juilliard, but they were very committed to bringing American music. Nobody in the quartet world had set out to bring Soviet music to Russia. But the time seemed right for us to show our sympathy with the plight of the Russian people by playing this music.

ROY LEWIS On our next two trips, we traveled to many of the different republics and we always got a very special response to Shostakovich, as if this vast audience were thanking us for recognizing their struggle.

DEXTER They also seemed to appreciate the fact that we made the effort to come at all. To travel where we went, like Kazakhstan, is not easy, even though we were taken care of very well by our embassy people.

Did you always play Shostakovich?

ERIC LEWIS Yes, but not exclusively. We also played American music. Guess what they *really* like, I mean, really, *really* like? [*Laughter.*]

Jazz?

ERIC LEWIS You're close: Jerome Kern.

Do you have arrangements of that?

ERIC LEWIS Yes, Kern and his arranger put them together for the Gordon String Quartet, and when we played "Smoke Gets in Your Eyes" for an encore, it was unbelievable. Everybody in the audience would recognize that tune, and they loved hearing it played by a string quartet.

Of course, everything sounds good for string quartet!

The St. Petersburg String Quartet

The prizewinning St. Petersburg String Quartet was formed in 1985 by graduates of the Leningrad Conservatory. They were mentored by Vladimir Ovcharek, first violinist of the Taneyev String Quartet, and were known as the Leningrad String Quartet until 1991, when their native city changed its name and the group followed suit.

The St. Petersburg is now in residence at the Oberlin Conservatory of Music in Ohio, where they have performed the complete cycle of Shostakovich's 15 string quartets. They are currently recording those works for the Hyperion label; the first CD in the cycle has just been released. The present members are Alla Aranovskaya, first violin; Ilya Teplyakov, second violin; Aleksey Koptev, viola; and Leonid Shukaev, cello. All but Koptev were with the group at the time of this 1997 interview.

For the Love of It

Russian musicians tend to refer to events and conditions in their homeland as "before" and "after," but when you ask how the differences have affected them, the answers vary according to age, professional status, and personal temperament. For example, the members of the Borodin Quartet (page 58), who recently celebrated the 50th anniversary of the group's founding, are steeped not only in a venerable musical tradition but also in the political climate of "before." Accustomed to expressing themselves with caution, especially to non-

Russian strangers, they insist on speaking through an interpreter even though several of them are fluent in other languages. They emphasize tradition when speaking about the past, and the practical rather than the ideological aspects of life when speaking about the present.

By contrast, the players of the St. Petersburg String Quartet belong to a very different, younger generation and talk much more freely about their problems and accomplishments. When I met them, I found that the cellist, Leonid Shukaev, and the second violinist, Ilya Teplyakov, spoke enough English to communicate directly with me and to translate for the other two players. This made for a fascinating conversation, though listening for the full meaning behind their words required an imaginative and empathetic ear.

I caught the players for the first time on a whirlwind visit to New York during a February cold spell that must have made them feel right at home. It was the start of what would prove to be a busy year for the quartet in this country—their schedule listed nearly 50 concerts from coast to coast. Their reason for coming to New York was the launching of their first recording on Sony Classical. Having already heard the record, which features the complete Tchaikovsky quartets, I knew that here was an arrestingly talented, promising group of high seriousness and dedication. The Russians have always been famous for a school of string playing, especially violin playing, distinguished by its singularly pure, beautiful sound and flawless technique. It seems to me that they are now also cultivating a school of quartet playing no less impeccable, both in terms of individual instrumental command and homogeneity of sound, intonation, ensemble, and expression. The St. Petersburg's tone is dark and warm, capable of nuance and variety. Their rhythm and pacing are supple and flexible; they take over lines and phrases seamlessly. Yet despite their technical perfection, they are not careful or inhibited but vibrantly human, with a youthful exuberance and romantic passion.

They are equally unconstrained in conversation. The first thing they tell me is that they have a brand-new violist: Konstantin Kats, who joined them last year. Andrei Dogadin, the fine violist on their record, had decided, as they put it, to change his musical life and play in an orchestra. "He competed for the position of principal violist in the Mavrinsky Orchestra, the first symphony orchestra in St. Petersburg, and won," Shukaev explains. "Of course, he had to give up playing in the quartet because it was impossible to combine both activities, so we invited Konstantin to play with us. We think the change has made the quartet stronger and helped it to reach a new level."

Shukaev was the moving force in trying to organize a quartet while still a student at the St. Petersburg Conservatory (then the Leningrad Conservatory). After two or three failed attempts, a group emerged in 1985 under the guidance of Professor Vladimir Ovcharek, first violinist of the Taneyev Quartet. In addition to Shukaev, the quartet included the present first violinist, Alla Aranovskaya, a leader with a virtuoso's flair and temperament. (In 1988, the original second violinist emigrated to Israel and was replaced by Teplyakov.) The group called itself the Leningrad Conservatory String Quartet, eventually dropping the "Conservatory."

In 1987, the quartet participated in two competitions in the USSR: the First International Shostakovich Competition for String Quartets in Leningrad, where it earned the "Laureate" title and won a special prize for best performance of the Shostakovich No. 7, the required work, and the All–Soviet Union String Quartet Competition in Voronezh, where they won First Prize. "That was a very hard competition," says Shukaev of the latter. "Quartets from many different republics of the Soviet Union participated, so the contestants were of a very high caliber."

I ask whether it is possible to establish a career in Russia without winning competitions. Without hesitation, they all agree that it is not; indeed, like most aspiring young performers, they have spent a lot of time on the competition circuit both at home and in the West. Their first opportunity to compete outside the USSR came in 1989, when they went to Tokyo for the Min-On International Competition of Chamber Ensembles and won the silver medal as well as a special prize. Next came the Vittorio Gui International Competition for Chamber Ensembles in Florence, where, they say proudly, they "won everything: first prize and two special prizes." One of the awards, the Sergio Meali Prize, was for the best piano-quintet performance. "We got it with the pianist Lyudmila Berlinskaya, the daughter of Valentin Berlinsky, cellist of the Borodin Quartet. The prize had not been given to anyone for 15 years," says Teplyakov.

Left to right, Konstantin Kats, Leonid Shukaev, Alla Aranovskaya, and Ilya Teplyakov.

Such competitions provided the only way for the quartet to travel outside the USSR and make contact with non-Russian musicians during the first three or four years of the group's career. "These connections were very interesting for us," the players say. "We listened to chamber-music concerts and not only heard other quartets, but had conversations with the players afterward, so we always learned something new."

In 1991, having changed its name to the St. Petersburg Quartet, the group took part in the prestigious International Competition for Chamber Ensembles in Melbourne, Australia, and brought back the First Prize and the Grand Prix Musica Viva. "The level of playing at that contest was as high as at the All-Soviet," the players say. "At all the other competitions, it was not as hard for us to win prizes."

As a result of these honors, the quartet began to get engagements in the USSR and abroad. They first came to America in 1989 to be artists in residence at the Musicorda Summer Festival and String Program in Massachusetts; they have returned there every summer since. Lately,

What they play

For the past three or four years, whenever the quartet has played in southern California, a local instrument collector has loaned them two violins, a 1714 Antonio Stradivari and a 1742 Giuseppe Guarneri del Gesù. The identities and origins of most of the quartet's own instruments are uncertain. Alla Aranovskaya plays a Tyrolean violin probably made in the beginning of the 19th century. Her bow is late–19th-century French, and she uses Pirastro Tonica strings with a Westminster Kaplan A. Ilya Teplyakov's violin was made by Charles Adolphe Maucotel in Paris in 1852. His bow is a modern Czech and he uses a Larsen A string; the rest are Pirastro Tonicas.

Leonid Shukaev plays a cello made in northern Italy in the mid-19th century. He also uses a modern Czech bow and his strings are Larsen, except for a Thomastik Spirocore C.

Konstantin Kats played a viola from early–20th-century Czechoslovakia. The new violist, Aleksey Koptev, plays an instrument with no label, although he says luthiers guess it is German, from the beginning of this century. His bow is a modern David Forbes and he uses a Larsen A string and a Spirocore D, G, and C.

"Our great dream," the players say, "is to get a whole set of instruments that's well-matched, healthy, without cracks, especially made for a quartet by the same maker—not necessarily one with a famous name. 'Before,' it was much easier to buy good instruments in Russia. Now the prices are enormous, much higher than in the West—we could not possibly afford them."

Recordings

Glazunov: Quartet No. 5, Five Novelettes (forthcoming on Delos).

Prokofiev: Quartets Nos. 1 and 2; Zurab Naderejshvli: Quartet No. 1 (Delos 3247).

Shostakovich: Quartets Nos. 2 and 3 (Hyperion CDA67153).

their schedule of U.S. appearances covers far more of the country, including Texas, Colorado, Arizona, California, and Hawaii.

"To have a career in Russia one must have concerts, good publicity, and success in the West," Teplyakov explains. "Musicians with great names, like [pianist Sviatoslav] Richter, do all right, but for young musicians, making a career is very difficult in Russia today."

More so than "before"? I ask. "Oh yes," says Shukaev. "Quartets cannot get regular work, just a concert now and then. We have no special managements or organizations for chamber music. Also, there are not many new quartets, because 'before,' conservatory students got good stipends to live on, but now the level of assistance is so low that something as difficult as building a quartet takes more time than they can afford to spend. They have to take every opportunity to work in orchestras and earn money to study. So it's a vicious circle."

"Above all," Teplyakov adds, "the government takes no interest in culture generally and classical music in particular. It is left to a few enthusiastic people to organize festivals and invite famous musicians; the cities have no policy of systematic involvement." When I ask if the government gives them any financial or promotional help, the answer is an emphatic "No!"

Teplyakov smiles. "The government helps us in just one way: by letting us play what we want," he says. "To my mind, that's help from the government. The situation is very simple. Sometimes concert organizers ask us if we would like to play in their hall; if we say yes, we discuss the program and go and play. The same happens at festivals. Or sometimes we tell the organizers that we would like to play a new program in their hall, or play with other musicians who interest us. But in Russia, concert organizations don't pay us. We play free concerts."

"We never take money," says Shukaev. "It's so little, we give it to the concert hall so they can make better publicity for other musicians, or for flowers." Amid laughter, Teplyakov elaborates, "In Russia, we play when we are interested, for the experience. Now, if the city government or an organization wants to pay us, it comes to $50 for the quartet." Appalled, I ask what they live on. Shukaev answers, "We [he and Aranovskaya] teach at the Conservatory, but even that does not pay enough. We do it because sometimes we have really talented students and that is interesting. It's when we play in the West that we get enough money to live on in Russia and play a free concert in St. Petersburg. But we never like to go on tour abroad for more than two months, because we don't want to leave our families."

The St. Petersburg's repertoire includes much of the standard Classical and Romantic quartet literature, as well as a number of piano and clarinet quintets. Of course they play a lot of Russian music, and in addition to the Tchaikovsky quartets, they have recorded both Borodin quartets and Shostakovich's Quartets Nos. 3, 5, and 7 for Sony Classical [these are now out of print]. Borodin's quartets are lush, romantic, song-

ful, and very Russian. The first is distinguished by a melancholy slow
movement and a Scherzo that sounds like chattering birds; the Trio creates a chiaroscuro of color by pitting harmonics against solid notes. The
second quartet is justifiably more popular; its most famous movement is
the Nocturne, a love song between cello and first violin on a beautiful
melody. The players give dignity and expressiveness to this music, which
could easily turn cheap and mawkish. Shostakovich's Fifth Quartet is
characteristically bleak, wild, and abrasive, a prolonged scream of agony
with some oases of resignation. The other two begin more cheerfully, but
the brightness soon turns dark, the light mood becoming wistful, sar-
donic, or tragic. The playing brings out all the
contrasts of texture and expression.

James Langone

The St. Petersburg's three-CD set of the complete Tchaikovsky works includes four very short
single movements and another more substantial
one—none of which I had ever heard before. I am
anxious to find out more about them. "Ah, it's
quite a story," Teplyakov says eagerly. "We received
an offer to record all the Tchaikovsky quartets
from the Dutch firm Etcetera, and they wrote us
that they had found these pieces in a catalog. So I
went to the special library in our Philharmonie

**Current members
(left to right) Alla
Aranovskaya, Ilya
Teplyakov, Aleksey
Koptev, and Leonid
Shukaev.**

and looked up many books about Tchaikovksy and discovered that he
had written the four short movements while he was a student at the
Conservatory, as an experiment in quartet writing; that's why they are so
short and so simple. When we got the parts, there were many, many mis-
takes in them, so as we rehearsed we changed some things a little, added
nuances, ritards, and so on—so some of the music is our work, not
Tchaikovsky's. It was very funny: when we recorded these four movements for the first time, our sound engineer listened and said, 'I don't
understand what you hear in this music, what you mean to say. I think
it should be different, maybe simpler.' So the next time, we played it
much more simply, and it was OK."

I ask about the one long movement. Did Tchaikovsky plan to make
a whole quartet out of it? "He wrote it twice," Teplyakov answers, "first
in three movements, but it was too long and he did not think it was
interesting enough. So he condensed it into one, in three parts: slow-fast-
slow." They have not performed any of these single pieces in public and
consider them of interest mostly for specialists and connoisseurs.

I tell them that their recording sounds wonderful. "You can thank
our sound engineer," says Teplyakov, eliciting laughter. "He is from St.
Petersburg, not young, but very experienced. He has worked with many
musicians. He is very important for us and a great help, a little like our
teacher. His name is Gerhard Tsess." They made the recording two years
ago. "Now, when we listen to it, we would like to change many things,"

Teplyakov says. "Of course, two years is a long time for a quartet: together we've become eight years older."

On the day after our conversation, at a luncheon hosted by Sony Classical, I have a chance to hear the group live. They play a movement from Shostakovich's First Quartet, the famous slow movement from the Borodin Quartet, and a Shostakovich polka in a scintillating arrangement. It quickly becomes clear to me that, although musically and technically their live performance is every bit as good as on the CD, their recorded sound does have a more rounded, shining quality than the real thing. This proves that good engineering can indeed make up for inferior instruments (see "What They Play," page 86). Unfortunately, their recording is played over the loudspeaker as background music before and after their performance, needlessly pointing up the contrast.

In July the quartet returns to New York near the end of their summer tour of the U.S. to perform a preconcert recital for the Mostly Mozart Festival at Avery Fisher Hall—during a record-breaking heat wave. It has accompanied them during their entire trip, but far from appearing wilted, they are in fine form. I gather from press reports that they received standing ovations everywhere, and indeed, they sound more integrated in tone and style than when I heard them in February. This is my first opportunity to hear the players performing non-Russian music: Haydn's Quartet Op. 20, No. 5. It is one of my favorites and they play it beautifully, bringing out all the subtle changes of mood, color, and expression; the final Fugue is both crystal-clear and menacingly mysterious. Shostakovich's Quartet No. 7 flows with the natural inevitability of a conversation in one's native language. Of course, the hall is much too big for these two intimate, delicate works, but the players' emotional involvement and projection cast a real spell. They deserve every success, at home and abroad, in concert and in the studio— including a set of fine, matched instruments.

"We have many musical plans," Teplyakov told me earlier. I hope they all materialize.

The Mendelssohn
String Quartet

The members of the Mendelssohn String Quartet are currently occupied as Blodgett Artists in Residence at Harvard University and as faculty members at the North Carolina School of the Arts. They also maintain a busy touring schedule and perform frequently in Europe as well as the United States.

The Mendelssohn's membership has changed substantially since this 1992 interview took place—and it's still changing as this book goes to press. Founding members still with the group are second violinist Nicholas Mann, son of former Juilliard Quartet violinist Robert Mann and an active recitalist and soloist who studied with Dorothy DeLay at Juilliard; and cellist Marcy Rosen, who is co–artistic director of the Eastern Shore Chamber Music Festival in Maryland, where the quartet is resident. Ulrich Eichenauer is now the group's violist; he was principal with the Dresden Philharmonic Orchestra and a teacher at the Musikhochschule in Detmold before joining the Mendelssohn Quartet. First violinist Nick Eanet, who replaced Ida Levin shortly after the following profile was written, has taken a position as concertmaster of the Metropolitan Opera Orchestra starting this season; the group is currently choosing a new violinist.

The Czech Connection

Photo by Christian Steiner

The Mendelssohn String Quartet, which recently celebrated its 13th anniversary, radiates so much unanimity of thought and spirit, both in performance and in conversation, that it is hard to believe only two of the players are founding members. The others are first violinist Ida Levin and violist Katherine Murdock. They are a dynamic, exciting group, distinguished by adventurous programming and a passionate, intense musical style. No wonder that, when our discussion momentarily went off on a culinary tangent, we decided that, in more than one sense, "the Mendelssohn Quartet cooks."

I was interested in asking them about the two remarkable quartets of Leoš Janáček, which they perform with remarkable authority and understanding. Janáček called his first string quartet "Kreutzer Sonata," after the story of jealousy and murder of the same name by Tolstoy. Janáček's second string quartet, which he called "Intimate Letters," was inspired by an autumnal passion for Kamila Stoesslova, a woman 30 years his junior, whom he met when he was 63 years old.

I want to know where you got your affinity for Czech music; I've heard you give some wonderful performances of Dvořák and also of Janáček, who is not generally so well-known.

LEVIN The fact is, we just like the music. We played Janáček's Second Quartet first, about four years ago, when I joined the quartet. I know that was the first piece of his I'd ever played, although I'd heard a lot of the others. Now we play the First Quartet as well; I'm sorry there aren't more. A few of us together have done the Concertino, and I'd love a chance to play the Sinfonietta one of these days.

ROSEN His music is so evocative and so unusual, there is no other composer who even slightly imitates him or whom he imitates. There is no resemblance in his writing to any other flavor of music.

Not any other Czech music? Do you feel there is no connection?

ROSEN Emotionally, yes, but not in sound and texture. It's fascinating, the way even his instrumental music has such a spoken quality.

Tell me, how do you play those fifths way up high in the Second Quartet?

LEVIN Oh, with . . . angles. You just sort of twist around. . . .

But to make them sound good! Everything is in so many flats. He must have loved that, but you have no open strings when you need them.

MURDOCK He does occasionally write things that are awkward. There are big climaxes where the bottom drops out, and it gets very treble-oriented.

How long did it take you to learn the quartets?

ROSEN Not too long. We try to start rehearsing a piece a least a month before we have to play it, which doesn't sound like very much, and we're not always successful with that endeavor. I think we actually started on the Janáček early in the month and then worked intensively the week before the concert.

LEVIN The tricky thing about these pieces isn't just putting them together, but making them feel organic, especially the tempo changes. It takes a long time till you're no longer saying in rehearsal, "Wait a minute, we've got this completely wrong," and realizing that *poco mosso* actually means that it's still slower than the previous tempo. You know, it's very complicated, the way he does that, and some of these tempos you just have to pick out of the air. So it's not until that becomes natural that you can really start playing around with it, and then you feel that you know the piece.

ROSEN And then you get to the point where you're incorporating the story into the music, and you no longer feel as if you're translating from one language into another. The music is written so programmatically that it becomes the story itself.

MURDOCK I listened to an old recording of the Smetana Quartet, and their tempos are very much slower and faster than the metronome markings. We take certain liberties, but this was just wildly different.

He puts in so many metronome markings—do they help or hinder?

ROSEN Well, it is certainly a great guide, because it gives you an idea of what he means when he says *poco mosso, poco* this, *poco* that.

MANN In the First Quartet, three of the movements are marked *Con moto.*

LEVIN Most of the metronome marks are "ca." [approximately]. And occasionally, in both quartets, there are misprints, where it's obvious he wrote the wrong number. From what I've read about his attitude toward his own music, I think he would have welcomed a fair amount of leeway.

MANN But a metronome mark never hurts, even if you end up throwing it out.

ROSEN We've worked with enough composers to know how rarely they are dogmatic about their own markings, tempo, dynamics—anything. When the composer is there, things can be so fluid; he'll hear something and say: "Well, let's try that a different way; it sounds a little fast." And we'll say, "But we really checked it with the metronome!" And he'll say, "It just sounds too fast."

Christian Steiner

Quartet members in 1993 (left to right): Marcy Rosen, Nick Eanet (who replaced Ida Levin), Nicholas Mann (front), and Katherine Murdock.

Do the transitions get easier just with time and playing, or have you found a way to rehearse and work them out?

LEVIN In the initial rehearsals, we actually stopped and hit the metronome, but the transitions come with performing rather than just playing separate movements. In the First Quartet, Janáček specified that he wanted the movements to be played with as little time in between as possible, so that the flow of the story doesn't get interrupted.

After all, that's the way Tolstoy reads—it's all just a nonstop narrative—and I guess Janáček wanted to preserve that continuity. Of course, you never get that in a rehearsal situation, but when you play the piece through, the feeling of going from one movement to the next alters the tempos a little.

MURDOCK At the beginning of the first movement, he wants you to put mutes on and off, and though there is actually no extra time allowed, it's really accounted for, rhythmically; you just add as much as you need.

LEVIN And every now and then he writes a little comment in Czech into the music.

Yes, and I'm really curious to know if you ever figured out what they mean.

LEVIN It's always something very pointed and poignant. There is the famous *vzdusne.*

What's that?

LEVIN I think it means light and airy—I looked it up once in a Czech dictionary. It became this funny byword for the group for a while: when we couldn't think of a way to describe how we wanted someone to play something, we'd say, "Just sort of *vzdusne.*" And then there's *spicky,* which wasn't in my dictionary but is obviously some kind of staccato, and *lkade,* which is like a lament. He probably felt using Czech words was the best way to explain what he wanted, but there are a couple I still don't know.

Is there literally a narrative line in the "Kreutzer Sonata" Quartet?

LEVIN Yes, from what I've read, I've concluded there really is. In the first movement, things are a bit vague, but the second movement is definitely supposed to be the violinist arriving on the scene, and then, when he and the wife are beginning to play together, you hear this tune that's very close to the real Beethoven "Kreutzer" Sonata, and then there is the stabbing, so there are certain clues. I gather Janáček left some letters indicating specific passages and also making a point about the stabbing not being the culmination of his story, as it is of Tolstoy's; he wanted the music to metamorphose into a sort of positive, optimistic ending, because that's how he felt.

The program of the "Intimate Letters" is even more vague. Are there any real clues to that?

LEVIN Well, there are some: the first meeting, between Janáček and Kamila, the summer they spent at the spa. . . . Each movement has a heading, and a sort of atmosphere.

And he did write a lot of letters to Kamila, didn't he?

LEVIN Yes, and it was his wife who sat on them for a long time, and the fact that "Intimate Letters" was all about Kamila didn't come out for a while, either.

But Janáček never made any secret of it.
LEVIN His wife knew, but she wasn't happy about it, that's for sure.

Though this so-called affair between him and Kamila was all in his imagination; there's a letter he wrote to her that leaves no doubt about it.
LEVIN Yes, I've read that.

He turned her into his muse who could rejuvenate and inspire him. His marriage was very unhappy. He'd lost his two children. And Kamila seems to have been a rather ordinary, simple person, who may have had no idea what all this agony and ecstasy were about.
LEVIN I'd like to believe there was more to it.

Christian Steiner

I'd rather believe there wasn't. She had two children, you know. It's nice to think of a passionate, elderly composer getting all fired up by his own feelings for a woman, without her doing anything at all to encourage it. And the music couldn't have been any better if the affair had been real.
ROSEN In fact, it might not have been as good.
LEVIN We'd love to record these quartets eventually; I think each of them can really stand on its own. I wouldn't want to hear them both in the same evening—they are too intense. We've thought of putting the "Kreutzer Sonata" together with the Dvořák A-Flat, for the Czech connection.

The group in 1999 (left to right): Nicholas Mann, new violist Ulrich Eichenauer, Nick Eanet, and Marcy Rosen.

Yes, I've heard you play that. Which of the other Dvořák quartets do you do?
MANN The C Major; the "American"; we did the "Cypresses," not the whole set, just seven of the 12; and we do the Two Waltzes, Op. 54.

I heard you play one of the waltzes, and you know, I heard another quartet play the same one for an encore just a few days before. That was the first time I'd ever heard it in public.
MURDOCK They were originally for piano, I think.

MANN There's also a string-orchestra version, written for a ball.

LEVIN The question we have is, what happened to Nos. 2 and 3? There are four in Op. 54, and Nos. 1 and 4 are arranged for quartet, so there must be two others somewhere.

What they play

Katherine Murdock has the oldest of the four instruments in the group, a Giovanni Paolo Maggini from 1600. "It was one of the four earliest instruments made to what is now considered a comfortable standard viola size, 16⅜ inches. It has double purfling, and I think it's a beautiful instrument," she says. The group's current violist, Ulrich Eichenauer, plays a contemporary viola by Peter and Wendy Moes of Connecticut.

Marcy Rosen's cello is a David Tecchler. "Did you see the Jacob Stainer exhibition that Jacques Français had at Lincoln Center several years ago?" she asks. "My cello was in that. But I wouldn't go see it there. I didn't want to see my cello sitting in a glass case!"

Nick Eanet plays a Giovanni Francesco Pressenda violin. Ida Levin has a J.B. Guadagnini violin made in Turin in 1781, and Nicholas Mann used to play a Guadagnini from the same period. Now he plays on an Antonio Stradivari—his second Strad.

"The rest of us helped him choose that instrument," says Rosen. "We decided among us that it sounded best with Ida's violin."

"It was interesting," adds Murdock, "because I was trying out my new viola just before that time and it was very different from the old one, so I was certainly disoriented. After this big change, Nicky came in with a Strad that had a completely different character from the previous one, so the whole quartet sound changed, perhaps more noticeably to us than to an outsider."

I ask how the players pick instruments that not only fit them as individuals, but also fit into the group. "Well," answers Levin, "the bottom line is that you have to be comfortable with the instrument you play. A good friend of mine is the first violinist of a quartet and is having absolute conniptions trying to decide between two violins; he likes one, and his partners unanimously prefer the other. They keep telling him to get the one he likes, because they are not terribly against it, but he's feeling very guilty, knowing they like the other one better."

"I tried one viola I really loved, but it just didn't work in the quartet at all," Murdock remembers. "I knew I wouldn't be happy having an instrument that sounded beautiful to myself under my ear but not in the group. It didn't have a distinctive voice; it blended so well that it disappeared."

"A quartet is really eight people: four players and four instruments," I comment.

"More—there are split personalities," responds Levin.

"Who," Mann asks, "the people or the instruments?"

"Oh, the people," Levin answers with a smile. "The instruments are very stable and secure."

I believe there are, but only for piano.

MANN I think Dvořák is still one of the most underrated composers. Just take the string quartets—they are played very rarely, except the "American," which is played to death. And of the symphonies, everybody picks the "New World," when there are so many others that are also wonderful.

ROSEN We played the E-Flat Quartet at our debut, and we've played the Sextet.

LEVIN And the Bass Quintet, with the Nocturne, the extra movement. When Simrock, his publisher, said it made the piece too long and told him to take it out, he set it for string orchestra and published it separately. There's also a version for violin and piano, and one for viola and piano. The Quintet is a fairly early piece, written originally as Op. 18, but when they published it without the Nocturne, they numbered it according to that time, as Op. 77, which is completely wrong.

Murrae Haynes

One of my greatest favorites is the Viola Quintet.

MANN Oh yes, that's beautiful.

LEVIN There is another viola quintet, Op. 1, but it's not very good.

MANN The early D-Minor Quartet that nobody ever plays is the piece he sent to Brahms, who thought very highly of it.

Then it should have great historical significance. I've always admired your wide-ranging, innovative programs. How do you select your repertoire?

ROSEN Most of the time we pretty much agree with each other about the repertoire we choose and how we make programs. Once a year we sit down with our individual wish lists, compare notes, decide how many programs we need to carry the following season—and very rarely does anyone come away disappointed. We always have another year for that one piece that won't fit! Since we have a series in New York at Merkin Hall every year, it often serves as the basis of our planning. For example, several years ago we did a performance of [Alberto] Ginastera's Third Quartet with soprano. We worked intensely on the piece with Mrs. Ginastera and felt a natural affinity with his music. This made us want to learn his first two quartets, and so we planned our Merkin series to do the complete Ginastera quartets.

MANN And we chose the three Tchaikovsky quartets to go with them. Most people think there is only one—the first quartet is the most

Former quartet member Ida Levin is now a soloist based in New York.

famous because of the slow movement, the beautiful Andante Cantabile. The others are rarely played, but they are wonderful pieces. Next season we're doing the three Brahms quartets coupled with the three by Schumann.

MURDOCK We're excited to play those programs, as exhausting as it will be!

ROSEN The question of programming is always interesting, and we give it a lot of thought. Certain auspices want specific kinds of programs—no contemporary music, all contemporary music, a guest artist, a piece by a board member's nephew. . . . We take all these things in stride as we decide how many new works to add to our repertoire each year. We do, however, believe strongly in commissioning works from composers of our choosing. Next season we will premiere two new string quartets that are being written for us right now. The Philadelphia Chamber Music Society, at our request, has commissioned composer Bernard Rands to write a piece for us that we'll premiere in Philadelphia in March of 1994, and we asked Augusta Reed Thomas to write a quartet for us that we'll premiere at Harvard, where we're in residence.

MURDOCK We're extremely fortunate in that regard. We've just begun a three-year tenure as the Blodgett Artists in Residence at Harvard. It's a visiting residency, and we spend four separate weeks there spread throughout the year. That keeps us very busy teaching and performing. Our colleagues are wonderful, and it's a very invigorating and inspiring atmosphere. This is in addition to our position at the University of Delaware, where we've been quartet in residence since 1989 [and where the group remained through 1997].

LEVIN The Delos Quartet had been in residence at Delaware for many years, but after they disbanded, a new chairman came in who was very keen on having a quartet. Since then, they hired a new president who is also very supportive, so we feel very secure, and very lucky, because we know that at this time many residencies are being eliminated. And we've learned that it's really essential for a quartet to have a position like this, as a sort of backbone to everything else.

MANN The string program in Delaware, beginning in the lower schools, has been severely hindered by state budget cuts, and we're doing our best to build it up. There's always support for the marching bands because of the football games, but string programs seem to come at the end of the list.

ROSEN Establishing a string program when nothing exists is very difficult. Our chairman and colleagues have been totally supportive in backing our efforts. Two years ago we started the Winter Institute for String Quartets, which takes place each January. It's an intensive week-long program where we coach preformed ensembles as well as at least one group that we put together from individual applicants. It's been a great success, and we've drawn students from all over this country and Canada. Our other activities at Delaware include tours throughout the state, music-appreciation classes, some graduate courses at the university, and a well-attended and very much-appreciated concert series. We feel lucky to have the musical support and financial backing of two such outstanding institutions.

MANN They understand that if their resident quartet is going to be successful, it will tour a lot, so they work out the schedule with us.

One more question concerning repertoire. Have you ever been asked to play a whole program of Mendelssohn quartets because of your name?

MURDOCK No, we haven't, and we don't really feel that would make the most interesting program, unless it were balanced with one of the quintets, perhaps.

MANN We're thinking about doing some sort of Mendelssohn event at some point, maybe in the form of an all-Mendelssohn recording. It's dangerous, being the Mendelssohn Quartet and not having a cycle ready!

ROSEN The closest we ever came to doing one was several years ago, when we coupled a cycle of the Schoenberg quartets with four Mendelssohn quartets.

Christian Steiner

Players (left to right) Mann, Murdock, Rosen, and Levin have coached numerous ensembles through their residency programs.

LEVIN I don't consider that we specialize in Mendelssohn, anyway; it just happens to be our name, and we love to play his music, but there are many other composers whose music is equally great. We're actually learning one Mendelssohn quartet right now that none of us has ever done, the E-Flat, Op. 44, No. 3.

ROSEN We've used the Scherzo for an encore, so now we're learning the rest of the piece. Audiences love it when we announce we'll play a little Mendelssohn for an encore; we did it a lot during our tenth-anniversary season. People are always asking us if we play Mendelssohn all the time, but we don't want to get stuck in a situation where it would be expected of us.

MANN There are a lot of questions that are asked of a young quartet. We used not to be able to walk from one person to the next without having to repeat the same answers: "Why is your name the Mendelssohn Quartet? Do you always play music by Mendelssohn? Why not?" That sort of thing. And slowly, as you get a little more established and the name is recognized, that changes. Nobody would go up to the Guarneri Quartet and ask, "Do you all play Guarneri instruments?"

Recordings

Antheil: Quartet No. 1 (MusicMasters 67094).

Davidson: Bleached Thread, Sister Thread (CRI 681).

Dvořák: String Quartet; Mendelssohn: String Quartet (MusicMasters 60102).

Mozart: String Quartets; Weber: String Quartets (MusicMasters 60177).

Picker: Quartet No. 1, "New Memories" (Electra/Nonesuch 79246).

Ran: Quartet No. 1 (Koch International Classics 7269).

Schoenberg: Quartet No. 1 in D Minor (MusicMasters 7015).

Toch: String Quartets, Opp. 26 70 (Laurel 850CD).

But to ask why you call yourselves the Mendelssohn Quartet, especially if you don't play his music all the time—that's a pretty fair question, isn't it?

ROSEN When our group was tossing names around, we came up with Mendelssohn because we all liked it, and because it fit all the criteria that were being required of any name we decided on.

What criteria?

ROSEN Well, the group was originally called the Hebrew Arts String Quartet, because it was formed by the Hebrew Arts School in New York—

LEVIN —which has recently been renamed the Lucy Moses Center for Music and Dance. We've had a continuous residency and annual concert series there all along.

ROSEN Anyway, when we first began, we didn't intend to become a real, live string quartet, we were just filling a small residency position, so we were quite happy with that name. Then, when we discovered that we enjoyed playing together and wanted to try to make a career of it, we really felt it wasn't a good name to be carrying as a banner, because it was too limiting; we'd have to play a lot of Hebrew art music, we wouldn't be able to play in Catholic schools, things like that. Well, the school wanted something that was connected with Judaism, and we often tell people we are named after Moses Mendelssohn.

Felix' grandfather, the philosopher? I'm afraid far fewer people would know about him than Felix!

ROSEN That's absolutely true. Anyway, the name fit, it satisfied everybody, and we convinced them that he was Jewish enough at one point in his life, and, technically, all his life.

MANN He was one of the most interesting musicians of his time, even apart from his compositions—his conducting, his discovery of Bach— so there's certainly no reason not to emulate him, as a person as well as a musician. And we do have eight pieces to fool around with; that's more than the Borodin or the Smetana Quartets can say. Another fringe benefit is that when people who don't know much about the music ask us, "What is your quartet?" and we say, "The Mendelssohn," they'll say, "Oh, I think I've heard of that. I'm sure that name sounds familiar."

The Orion
String Quartet

Since it was formed in 1987, the Orion String Quartet has become one of the most impressive and admired groups of its kind, and this 1994 interview clearly reveals the players' extraordinary adaptability and adventurous spirit. They are in residence at the Mannes College of Music and the Chamber Music Society of Lincoln Center, and to celebrate the new millennium, the Society is sponsoring their presentation of the complete Beethoven Quartets, in six concerts at Alice Tully Hall. Those pieces represent a milestone for any quartet—as the group's cellist, Timothy Eddy, says, "That's what quartet playing is really all about, isn't it?"

In addition, the Orion is undertaking an outreach program with six community institutions that offer musical instruction to children; their first visit was to the Harlem School of the Arts in October 1999. The players are waiving their fee for all of these activities, and the series of concerts, in May 2000, will be free to the public.

Star Power

H alf of the Orion String Quartet was a gift of nature: its two violinists, Todd and Daniel Phillips, are brothers who come from a large family of musicians and have played together all their lives. Their father, also a violinist, was in the Pittsburgh Symphony for many years, "but he never imposed music on us as a profession," says Todd. "He just wants it to be part of everybody's life. When Danny was born, he brought a little violin and introduced it into his cradle. He used to play sonatas with our mother, who is a pianist, and he's also a composer. We performed his first string quartet last season, and he wrote a wonderful duo for the two of us, and a song cycle for our sister, who's a singer." Best of all, the elder Phillips had a string quartet in which each of his sons played second violin (Todd took over when his older brother Daniel went to college). The brothers have always known that they wanted to play quartets, and so, in 1987, the Orion Quartet was born.

How did they find the other half of the group? Their cellist, Timothy Eddy, says he and Daniel Phillips "developed a long relationship over the years, playing in the Bach Aria Group and at various festivals. Actually, at one point the three of us were playing together and quietly trying each other out." Their original violist was Catherine Metz, formerly of the Primavera Quartet, and when she left this season, Steven Tenenbom, whom they had known and played with for years in many other situations, took her place. "It wasn't like playing with a new person at all," says Todd Phillips. "That's why he is such a wonderful, natural addition to the quartet."

Tenenbom, for his part, is delighted to be their partner. "It was great for me to come into this group because, after five years or so, a quartet has established its direction, its sound, and its character, and I felt these guys had already done all that groundwork."

Daniel Phillips explains, "Of course, the dynamics are different with different people, but we just sat down and rehearsed with Steve the way we always had. He said what he thought, and we sometimes admitted that we were doing certain things simply because we were used to them; luckily we don't mind making changes."

Collaborating with different partners is second nature to these players, and they are justly proud of their adaptability. They are all busy soloists with extensive experience in chamber music. Tenenbom, for example, plays with Tashi, a mixed ensemble of strings and winds, and both he and Timothy Eddy were members of the Galimir String Quartet, in residence at the Mannes College of Music until Felix Galimir retired. When Eddy first joined the Orion Quartet, he played concurrently in both groups—an extraordinary feat, demanding the utmost flexibility and sensitivity, since two more dissimilar groups can hardly be imagined (the former led by a veteran pioneer and bearer of a long tradition collaborating with three highly accomplished younger players; the latter newly formed by a group of peers).

"I admit I was a little worried at first," Eddy says, when asked how he managed the adjustment. "But then I thought, every time you sit down to play chamber music, whether it's string quartets or something else, the circumstances are different. We've all played chamber music in a variety of settings, and the ability to free ourselves from our own preconceptions, to give each other space to find our way and make each collaboration unique, is part of being an experienced musician. Though we may bring our habits and associations to a piece, we try, as we play and listen, to react to it *now*, with these particular people, because it's going to feel and sound different. Another very important thing is that a group is created primarily in rehearsal, where one of the basic skills is knowing when to speak up, when not to speak up, when to bring up what kind of subject, how long to persevere with it, and so on. And I find that I ultimately benefit tremendously from trying to balance being open to others with asserting myself, both in rehearsal and performance."

This openness is part of the quartet's character. The violinists, in a spirit of true brotherly sharing, trade parts because they enjoy the variety and "because it cuts down the pressure of having to learn all those notes in the first violin parts," says Todd Phillips. "Playing second is less demanding technically, but harder in other ways: you've got to have your wits about you, keep your antennae out all the time."

What made them decide to alternate? They laugh. "Having to decide who'd play first would have been worse," says Daniel. "We don't really care too much about who plays first on which piece. We just want to lead half of a program each: one big piece or two shorter ones. Then we'll reverse it on another program, so it evens out in the end."

Suppose both want to lead the same piece? They grin. "That hasn't happened yet."

Todd sighs when asked whether alternating makes it more difficult to plan programs. "Well, it can be complicated, especially when concert organizers make certain conditions, or when we share programs with other players. Then it does not work out as perfectly as we'd like, but if we can have a balance over the whole season, it's good enough." Tenenbom's question, "We wouldn't turn down a concert because of that, would we?" makes everybody laugh.

Orion members (left to right) Timothy Eddy, Daniel Phillips, Steven Tenenbom, and Todd Phillips.

When the players started out, they also experimented with different seatings, sometimes placing the violins side by side, sometimes facing each other, while the cello and viola alternated between the inside and outside seats of the quartet. The choice was dictated by style and balance. "You get more of a sense of dialogue, of separation, between the violins across the stage, while in unisons or fast runs in the thirds together, it's clearer the other way," the brothers explain.

Tenenbom likes the inside seat. "I have a good view of both violinists, and I don't have to turn my viola out the way I do on the outside," he explains.

Eddy says, "I was so accustomed to sitting in the back, with the viola outside next to me, that when my colleagues first started talking about playing musical chairs, I was very resistant to changing. I had not expected the advantages of the other positions, but I soon discovered that each had distinct characteristics, and playing the same pieces in various ways has given me, and I'm sure all of us, different perspectives on the music and the whole art of making a quartet work. Sitting next to the first violin is terrific in setting up the frame of a composition by

What they play

Daniel Phillips has a 1702 Stradivari. He doesn't know what happened to its original scroll, which was replaced with a new one in 1980 at Charles Beare's shop in London. His bow is a Simon-Vuillaume; his strings are Dominant A, D, and G, and a Westminster E. Todd Phillips also plays a Stradivari, made in 1732 and called the "Wiener-Busch." It was played by Adolf Busch and is on loan from his family. His bow is by Persois; his strings are a Dominant G, D, and A, and a Westminster E. The E strings were recommended to them by the New York restorer René Morel as having a particularly strong, full sound.

Both brothers use chin rests designed and constructed by their father; made of beautiful olive wood, "they are higher than most, which can eliminate the need for a shoulder rest, and they set your chin closer to the center of the instrument, where many people actually hold it," Daniel says.

Steven Tenenbom's viola is very unusual and he speaks about it knowledgeably and eloquently. "It's a Gasparo Da Salò of 1560—compared to its age, the guys' violins are just babies." It measures 18¼ inches, an enormous length. "Most instruments that size have been cut down; this is the largest uncut, vintage Da Salò. The viola was originally called a tenor and, acoustically speaking, its length should be about 22 or 23 inches. As technical demands increased, some of that size and resulting resonance were sacrificed for ease of playing, and it became an alto. But I've always liked the sound of the large instruments, though I must admit they are very taxing to play. I really have to contort myself to get my hand around those wide shoulders, that big body. The advantage of playing on such a difficult instrument has been to make me extra careful to be relaxed; if I allowed any tension to develop—which on a smaller instrument I might not notice until it was too late—I'd end up in the hospital very quickly." The string length is the same as on a normal 16-inch viola, because in Da Salò's Brescian style, the bridge and f-holes are differently placed than in the Cremonese style of Stradivari. The viola bow is a Sartory; the strings are all Helicores.

Timothy Eddy's cello is a Matteo Gofriller of 1728, recently restored by René Morel; his bow is a Dominique Peccatte that, because of the shaping of the inside surface of the tip, is called a Swanhead. The cello strings are a Jargar A and D (steel) and a Spirocore silver-wound G and C.

having the top and the bottom voice next to each other, and it's also easier for me to feel in touch with the viola."

Daniel Phillips adds, "When you're playing complicated inner parts,
it's important to have the inner voices close together."

A couple of years ago, they settled on a configuration used by many
quartets around the turn of the century, with the violins facing each
other, the cello behind the first, and the viola behind the second violin.
"We got tired of moving around; I might change places three times in
one concert," says Daniel Phillips.

"And find another guy's music on your stand," murmurs Tenenbom.

"But with Steve coming into the group," says
Todd Phillips, "we may start experimenting again.
He didn't mind our seating because he's very
accommodating, but perhaps he'll want to try the
other one sometimes and get some feedback from
the people who listen to us."

Nora Feller

The quartet has even involved audiences by
asking for reactions to various seatings within one
program. "We took a vote once and it was split
right down the middle," says Eddy. "But it was
great, because it got people all stirred up listening, thinking, discriminating."

The Orion Quartet first appeared in New York
at the 92nd Street YMHA in 1989, in an extremely impressive and successful debut. "We were
lucky," says Daniel Phillips. "We had management
before we had a quartet. When I told Barrett
Management, with whom I was signed up as a soloist, that I was planning to have a string quartet, they said they wanted to manage it as soon
as it existed. So we were able to bypass one of the nasty first steps faced
by most quartets."

**The players like to
experiment with
repertoire and seating,
and the two violinists
regularly trade parts.**

In the years since that auspicious beginning, the Orion has more
than fulfilled its promise, firmly establishing itself as one of the most
sought-after, as well as accomplished and interesting, string quartets.
The group's technical virtuosity, musical freedom, and expressive power
seem to grow each time I hear it. (Its name, which the players say they
picked mostly by chance, later turned out to carry symbolic significance: Orion is the constellation in which most new stars are said to be
formed.) They present a series of concerts at the Gardner Museum in
Boston, and, in addition to their American tours, they are increasingly
in demand in Europe and have several European managers.

One interesting project was a collaboration with the Guarneri
Quartet (see page 112). "We did a program of mixed ensembles," says
Todd Phillips. "No string quartets, but a viola quintet, a sextet, and the
Mendelssohn Octet. It was fabulous, a great experience for us, and they
seemed to enjoy it too, so we hope we can do it again in the future."

The Orion has been quartet in residence at the Spoleto Festival in Italy, where its first summer, in 1989, was "a kind of work retreat," says Eddy. "It was an extremely valuable time: we could work intensively without the usual distractions of our winter lives, and there was a concert every day, shared with a pool of players, which meant performing together steadily." The players went back two summers later. They are still in residence at the Spoleto Festival in Charleston and also at the Santa Fe Chamber Music Festival, where they are presenting a Bartók cycle over two years.

In 1994, they were appointed to two new residencies: at Mannes College, where they took over from the Galimir Quartet, and at the Chamber Music Society of Lincoln Center. Of the latter, Eddy says, "We're delighted about that association and look forward to it very much. We're playing on three of their regular concerts, some of which are also performed in Washington; on their contemporary-music series; and we're also doing some children's concerts." Each program will include a string quartet and collaborations with members or guests of the Society.

Chris Nail

The Mannes College residency places the quartet members on the faculty but primarily requires them to give a series of four concerts a year and conduct public master classes as a quartet. "This means that all four of us are in the concert hall; we hear a group play and all of us can, and do, comment," Eddy explains.

The players had a strong connection to violinist Felix Galimir (1910–99), who taught them at the Curtis Institute and the Marlboro Festival.

Tenenbom nods and adds, "That's how we did it with the Galimir Quartet, but we found that the best way to deal with the situation was for one person to take over, more or less; then the others could reinforce the same ideas or add different ones. Otherwise, there could easily be chaos. We'll see how the dynamics work with the four of us."

Taking over the Mannes College residency from Felix Galimir means coming full circle for the Orion players: Tenenbom had studied with Galimir at the Curtis Institute in Philadelphia, and the Phillips brothers and Eddy all studied with him at the Marlboro Festival. They speak of him with an affection bordering on veneration. Tenenbom says, "I always loved doing master classes with Felix, because I loved listening to him. He has an incredible ear and a special way of working with an ensemble. When I was studying with him, I realized that the more he cared, the more animated and demanding he became. But even if he yelled at you, it was always in a loving way."

Todd Phillips agrees. "Everybody loves him; he has such a warm, charming personality. Wherever he goes, he's always surrounded by students and friends."

Eddy also acted as coach in workshops for ensembles conducted recently by violinist Isaac Stern with other formidable chamber-music luminaries, such as members of the Guarneri Quartet, violinist Henry Meyer of the LaSalle Quartet, and pianists Claude Frank, Leon Fleischer, and Joseph Kalichstein. Eddy describes the dynamics of that situation as "very complex, because the teachers were reacting not only to the students but to each other. I personally was fascinated by hearing what my colleagues were saying, and also by the challenge of figuring out when to speak up and when to be quiet."

Tenenbom remarks, "I've always felt that the best approach in any master class is to focus on a few concise points and let the students come away with a limited but concentrated amount of information. With several teachers coaching, it can get awfully confusing to the students if four or five people are each making one or two points."

"There is that danger, but the variety of ideas and opinions can also be very valuable," Eddy responds.

The members of the quartet teach a lot. "We're devoted to it," says Daniel Phillips, who is on the faculty at Queens College and at the State University of New York at Purchase. Eddy is at SUNY Stony Brook and Tenenbom is at the Hartt School in Hartford, and they also often conduct master classes.

So how much can students benefit from a one-time exposure to a visiting teacher, usually in a public setting with a roomful of listeners? "Of course, such a format is only an adjunct to weekly lessons or coaching with a regular teacher; it can never take its place," says Eddy. "But one hopes to give the participants something of lasting value. One of the most exciting things is to see how much actual change you effect in their playing, right then and there, without letting them go home and work it out. Achieving a new or higher degree of success often goes beyond their own expectations, and when it's unmistakable to the whole audience that something wonderful has just happened, the dimension of the response has much more impact on the students than the same experience in a private lesson.

The Orion has residencies at both the Mannes College of Music and the Chamber Music Society of Lincoln Center.

"Now from my own point of view as a teacher, these public master classes are always fascinating, a real adventure, because you have no idea what to expect," Eddy goes on. "Sometimes I've found myself at a loss and getting nervous, either because I hear something that doesn't sound quite right but can't figure out what it is, or what to say or do about it, or because the student sounds excellent and I can't think of any suggestions to offer."

Recordings

Dvořák: "American" Quartet; Piano Quintet. With Peter Serkin, piano (Arabesque Z6731).

Marsalis: String Quartet No. 1, "At the Octoroon Balls"; A Fiddler's Tale Suite. With Wynton Marsalis, trumpet; David Schifrin, clarinet; Milan Turkovic, bassoon; David Taylor, trombone; Ida Kavafian, violin; Edgar Meyer, bass; Stefon Harris, percussion (Sony Classical 60979).

Mendelssohn: Quartet No. 3 in D Major, Op. 44, No. 1; Octet for Strings in E-Flat Major, Op. 20. With the Guarneri String Quartet (Arabesque Z6714).

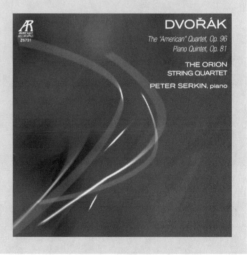

Clearly, one of the quartet's most striking characteristics is the members' openness to change, experimentation, and ideas. Eddy attributes this attitude to "our curiosity, our appetite for learning, our desire to grow as musicians. Anyone who tries to put together a string quartet must sometimes wonder, why are we going to all the trouble of doing this? And one of the central reasons is that the string quartet holds out to the player an experience unlike any other, in terms of the literature, of understanding the medium itself, and of what it can teach us about music and string playing. Whatever the rhythm of our concert activities—and of course we want as many concerts as we can sustain—the real focus of our concern and excitement is that we're building our repertoire and developing as a group."

The Orion's latest projects range from performing the complete Beethoven quartets to recording with trumpeter Wynton Marsalis.

The Guarneri
String Quartet

The Guarneri String Quartet, interviewed here in 1992, was formed in 1964 at the Marlboro Festival, with the encouragement of Alexander Schneider, violinist of the Budapest String Quartet. The four original members, violinist Arnold Steinhardt, second violinist John Dalley, violist Michael Tree, and cellist David Soyer, are all still with the group, making it one of the most stable quartets ever. However, in late 1999, Soyer announced that he would be curtailing his activities and playing with the group only on the East Coast; his protégé Peter Wiley has begun taking his place in all other concert locations.

Party of Four

As one of the preeminent groups of its kind, the Guarneri String Quartet has been the subject of innumerable interviews and several books, and it has been written about from so many different points of view that few general topics of discussion have been left uncovered. When I met with the group, I therefore suggested exploring, among other things, a few specific areas especially on my mind and related to recent events: Arnold Steinhardt's absence from the quartet for half a season because of a playing injury, and what this meant for him and the quartet; and the quartet's famously contentious rehearsal process, which was highlighted by the release of a documentary film called *High Fidelity* (directed and produced by Allan Miller), a title with a clever double meaning, since the quartet has been together for so many years. The film (which observes the players rehearsing, performing, recording, touring, and spending time with their families) provoked strong reactions; I was troubled by its almost unrelieved emphasis on the negative aspects of their relationship, especially the unresolved dissension in rehearsal scenes.

These topics were indeed a road less traveled, and although we all realized that they could lead us into dangerously sensitive territory, the quartet agreed to pursue them with me, and their openness and generosity made all the difference.

Playing injuries are certainly of interest to all of us who have done battle with the effects of short- or long-term disabilities. In your case the situation must have been particularly serious because it affected the whole quartet. I am eager to talk about this, and I'm sure there are hundreds of other people who would be grateful to read about it.

STEINHARDT Well, progressively, for ten years, I had pressure on a nerve in my left arm around the elbow. It's a rather common ailment. I found that a lot of musicians, many violinists, have it. Some very famous ones have had operations for it; the most notable of these was Joseph Fuchs, who had one of the first ones ever performed. I went along for ten years without any of that, but it slowly got worse. I was losing some of the strength in my left hand because of it, and about three and a half years ago it finally got severe enough for the doctors to think it warranted surgery. I got my strength back—pretty much—and a couple of months later I came back and we played; I sort of eased back into the season.

But ever since then, the elbow has always been rather tender and prone to inflammation, and I have to be careful about it. So eventually it got inflamed and it bothered me for quite a while, but being a quartet, the four of us are joined at the hip, so to speak, so there are all kinds of things to weigh, even though it's not nice to play injured. But finally it got bad enough for me to go and see some doctors, and we all felt that a rest was appropriate. So while I was resting, the quartet carried on without me through almost every single concert of the first part of the season, playing string trios and piano trios and wind quartets with guests. It was a really heroic operation.

How far ahead of time did you know that all the programs would have to be changed?

DALLEY I heard about it the last part of August, at the very end of the summer. I made an about-face. My manager said, "You have to play this and this and this, so you hurry and scurry and grab the old parts that you played maybe once or twice years ago, and refamiliarize yourself with them."

How long did you have to prepare those programs?

SOYER We did normal rehearsals. We play some of those works constantly throughout the season, because at our series in Tully Hall we always have guest artists.

STEINHARDT Not only that, but we have a policy of occasionally inserting a string trio into our traveling programs, so *that* repertoire is not unknown to the group, either. Still, it must have been tough.

Could you predict how long you would be laid off?
STEINHARDT No.

So you just went from concert to concert?
TREE We just went from day to day.

When you started to play again, did you find some technical skills had been lost faster than others and were harder to regain?
STEINHARDT Not really. People have warned me that when you get older your body is no longer as resilient and you should never stop practicing, not even for a vacation. But I've always taken a vacation in the summer for a week or two.

But isn't there a difference between a real vacation and an enforced one?
STEINHARDT This was just a longer one. It was a strange feeling in that you realize how much of your life revolves around not only playing concerts and making music, but also the tactile sense of working with an instrument, and being without that was disorienting for a while. On the other hand, it was really quite marvelous to be free. But

Dorothea von Haeften

coming back—in a certain sense this sounds terrible, but it's like riding a bicycle. Once you learn how to do it, you can always do it. When you start again, you pick up the instrument and everything works, you can play. But only for a couple of minutes; then you find that all your muscles have turned to blubber.

Guarneri members (left to right) Michael Tree, David Soyer, John Dalley, and Arnold Steinhardt.

Do some things come back faster than others?
SOYER Fear—fear comes faster [*laughter*].

STEINHARDT It's just like an athletic ability. If you've run a mile all your life and then you've stopped for half a year, you have to work back up to it gradually.

DALLEY Athletes just accept the fact that they have to stop at a certain, arbitrary point; their career ends, it's gone. But as a musician, you have to keep on going. So it's a matter of tricking your body or learning somehow to live with it, because you don't really want to stop playing.

STEINHARDT Somebody asked Jascha Heifetz in an interview, "You're the greatest violinist in the world. Why don't you play the Paganini Concerto?" And he said, "I used to play it when I was very young, but I no longer feel that my technique is reliable enough." Heifetz said that!

TREE In some ways the string-quartet literature is more difficult than the Paganini Concerto. We often listen to young players audition for Curtis, or Marlboro, or the New York String Orchestra Seminar. These

What they play

Arnold Steinhardt plays a late–18th-century Lorenzo Storioni violin from Cremona, Italy. John Dalley's violin is a Nicholas Lupot from France, 1810. Michael Tree's viola was made by Domenico Busan in Venice, 1750. And David Soyer's cello is a Ferdinand Gagliano from Naples, 1778.

Christian Steiner/PHILIPS CLASSICS PRODUCTIONS

kids—there are a hundred of them around New York who can play the Sibelius Concerto in their sleep, perfectly, and then you put a Mozart Quartet in front of them—not to sight-read, but one they came prepared to play—and suddenly, nothing works. The melody is out of kilter, the wrong notes are accentuated, they can't play in tune, their shifts are in the wrong places, they even get tangled up in the runs. The whole mechanism falls apart.

STEINHARDT That's true of Bach, too; a kid who can play a concerto wonderfully comes to Bach and you'd swear it's not the same violinist, because Bach calls for something else; it's music, not showing off.

[Author's note: During the 1991–92 season, the quartet has continued to program string trios, and works with guests, in which Arnold Steinhardt does not participate. The two violinists have also begun to trade the first and second parts, and Dalley frequently takes the lead in works that are either being revived after a long time or added to the repertoire. To me, it is fascinating that even partners of such long standing can reveal new dimensions in the ensemble by a change of roles. The differences between the two violinists, both instrumental and musical, have become more apparent, yet they still both blend with and complement one another, as each of them brings out the respective characteristics of his part in his own way. Also, there is something bracing and exciting in the subtle changes of interaction between all four players caused by the different constellations, which adds depth and breadth to their performances. Shortly before this interview, the quartet played Mozart's Horn Quintet with Tree on violin, Dalley on first viola, and Steinhardt on second viola.]

Isn't it risky to switch between violin and viola?

STEINHARDT You mean physically? No. In one way, the viola is probably easier for me, because the angle of the elbow is more comfortable; but then, the fingers need more strength. Anyway, all three of us are violinists as well as violists; we've all played viola for more than half of our lives. It's not totally new territory.

TREE At the Curtis Institute, where the three of us were students, every violinist played viola for a year; that was required in the curriculum.

But to switch at a concert?

DALLEY It can be troublesome, that's true, although many fine players do it a lot: Oscar Shumsky, Pinky [Zukerman], Jaime [Laredo].

STEINHARDT I don't find the transition hard at all. I think it's hard to play the violin well, and it's hard to play the viola well, but if you learn pieces you perform thoroughly, on each instrument, then, for me, the transition is almost immediate.

TREE I think it's a very healthy thing. There are some players, particularly violists, who might disagree, because their point of view is that you're either a violinist or a violist, and if you want to be a violist, you should devote your life to it. I've spoken to a number of very well-known violists to whom it's almost an emotional question; they feel very strongly against violinists playing viola. But I don't agree with them; I think both fiddle players and violists should interchange. It's very interesting for both. Let me mention that there's a wonderful piece by our friend George Perle, a partita for unaccompanied violin and viola; it's in five movements and three of them are for viola. It should be played more often.

Changing instruments is not the only unusual thing you do. I've noticed, especially lately, that you don't seem to use the same bowings much of the time.

DALLEY We are more interested in sounding good than in looking the same.

TREE Occasionally we'll talk about bowings, but generally we don't even bother, unless something sounds very different because of a change of bow, like stresses or accentuations. But otherwise I think we're the most uncaring of quartet players.

DALLEY Well, we're more practical. We realize that the same stroke doesn't always sound good for all four of us, so sometimes there's a conscious effort just to maintain a good sound, like playing a unison on different strings; sometimes you feel you can play better with another person with a slightly different bow stroke, or a different up-down. Some years ago, the quartet was asked to put out an edition of the Beethoven quartets, so each of us took his own part and put his markings in it. Since none of them were the same, the result was utter confusion, and people couldn't believe what they were seeing. We finally concluded that what you do on stage cannot be put down on a piece of paper and codified for consumption.

Over the years you've played together, have you found that you no longer need to rehearse as much?

TREE With something like the Beethoven Quartets, no matter how often one has played them, it takes a lot of work every time. We just recorded the complete Beethoven Quartets for Phillips; the middle and late ones have already been released. This is our second recorded cycle; the first one was for RCA Victor, about 20 years ago. I understand that we are the only American quartet to have recorded the Beethoven cycle twice with the same personnel.

Didn't you also make a lot of recordings with [pianist] Arthur Rubinstein?

STEINHARDT Yes, we played and recorded ten pieces with him, and there are certain phrases that I'm still waiting for somebody to do better than he did. He just put his signature on them; it was remarkable.

You've also played with other wonderful guests. Can you tell me how one homogenizes another player into a quartet?

DALLEY There are three types of guest artists: Those who take over a rehearsal and you quickly realize that you must follow, must go with that person, for various reasons, and that's the way it happens in public. The second kind is the one who joins the quartet and you're not aware that somebody has come in. It's like a glove, fitting perfectly on your hand. [Pianist] Seymour Lipkin is like that; it's like another string player joining the group. And the third type is the one who presents a picture of one sort of player in rehearsal and then does something entirely different on stage.

STEINHARDT I'll add a fourth one—the type who's young and inexperienced and thinks that chamber music is such a holy thing, they're too scared to play.

SOYER Then there's the kind who come in having learned a piece the way we did it on the recording and are amazed that we're not playing it like that.

STEINHARDT But sometimes something wonderful happens. We played with Stanley Drucker, the first clarinetist of the Philharmonic, and he was very good at the rehearsals, but at the concert, everything was entirely different. Afterward I said to him, "Stanley, that was fantastic, but it was so different!" And he said, "Yes, the rehearsals were for the public; the concert was for you."

What did he mean?

STEINHARDT He didn't want us to get bored with his playing, so at the concert he did something else, to stimulate us in a slightly different way, and I found that very refreshing.

Cellist Peter Wiley is taking over for David Soyer in East Coast concert performances.

It takes a great deal of trust in the ensemble to do that.

DALLEY Yes, it does. I think when people come into the group, they sense immediately how much they can do, and we sense that, too. For example, with [pianist Arthur] Rubinstein, who was very commanding, we sensed that we had to be right there with him, follow him, to make it successful—and that was fine.

Do you pick your partners or does the management hand them to you?

TREE We pick them.

DALLEY We auditioned Rubinstein [*laughter*]. . .

TREE Musicians who have played with us have felt that we're sometimes a bit more gruff than they are used to; they tell stories about us being tough guys. But we're really not, we're teddy bears. We're very easy to get along with; it's just that we have to get a lot done in too little rehearsal time.

Recordings

Juan Crisostomo de Arriaga: *String Quartets Nos. 1–3 (Philips).*

Beethoven: *Grosse Fuge String Quartet (Philips 422059).*

Beethoven: *Complete String Quartets, Nos. 1–6, Op. 18 (RCA 3 60456).*

Beethoven: *Complete String Quartets, Nos. 7–11, Opp. 59, 74, 95 (RCA 3 60457).*

Beethoven: *Complete String Quartets, Nos. 12–16, Opp. 127, 130–132, and 135 (RCA 3 60458).*

Beethoven: *Quartets, Nos. 1–6 (Philips 434115).*

Beethoven: *Quartets, Nos. 7–9 (Philips 432980).*

Beethoven: *Quartet No. 10, "Harp"; Quartet No. 14 (Philips 422341).*

Beethoven: *Quartet No. 11, "Quartetto serioso"; Quartet No. 15 (Philips 422388).*

Beethoven: *Quartet No. 12, Quartet No. 16 (Philips 420926).*

Beethoven: *Quartet No. 13 (Philips 422059).*

Debussy: *String Quartet; Ravel: String Quartet (RCA Silver Seal 60909).*

Dvořák: *Quartet No. 12, "America"; Piano Quintet, Op. 81. With Arthur Rubenstein, piano (RCA 6263).*

Mozart: *Quartets Nos. 14 and 15 (Philips 426240).*

Mozart: *String Quintet, K. 174; String Quintet, K. 516. With Ida Kavafian, violin; Steven Tenenbom, violin (RCA Red Seal 7770).*

Mozart: *String Quintet, K. 406; String Quintet, K. 593. With Ida Kavafian, violin; Steven Tenenbom, violin (RCA Red Seal 7771).*

Mozart: *String Quintet, K. 515; String Quintet, K. 614. With Ida Kavafian, violin; Kim Kashkashian, violin (RCA Red Seal 7770).*

Schubert: *Quartet No. 13, "Rosamunde"; Quartet No. 14, "Death and the Maiden" (Arabesque 6887).*

Let me ask you about that film, High Fidelity. *It left me very dissatisfied, because, as you know, I am a great admirer and loyal fan of the quartet. I think what troubled me most was the rehearsal scenes. They showed nothing except disagreements, and never how they are resolved.*

SOYER What did you expect to see us do in rehearsal? Agree? Then we would have nothing to say. It's in the nature of rehearsals to be negative. We don't say, "That was very good, let's do it that way." It's always, "No, let's not do it that way."

I would have liked to find out whether the things you disagree about change in the course of time, and whether agreement comes more easily.

DALLEY That depends. If it's about somebody's personal way of playing something, that might be carried over from year to year. But if it's of a very practical nature, where you have to agree on a certain way of doing something, it depends on how much time you have. If you have a lot, you can argue ad infinitum, but if you have to get through a certain number of works in one rehearsal, then at the concert you just go ahead and do it.

STEINHARDT These issues are resolved in rehearsal; we don't just disagree and leave. We talk and we agree, otherwise it would be chaos on stage. So if we disagree on, say, whether a phrase should have a ritard or not, we will argue about it and decide, even if one or two of us are unhappy about the result, "OK, I don't like the ritard, but if that's your point of view, let's try it tonight." So we try it, and then often the proof is in the pudding. It becomes much clearer in performance than in rehearsal whether something is convincing or not.

Violinist Arnold Steinhardt's book is an affectionate portrait of the career of the Guarneri Quartet.

[Author's note: The quartet has become a remarkable musical and social unit over the decades, and its history is affectionately recounted in a 1998 book by Steinhardt, Indivisible by Four: A String Quartet in Pursuit of Harmony *(Farrar Straus Giroux, New York). As Steinhardt said shortly after its publication, he wrote the book to answer such common questions as, "How do you stay together with the same people for so long, especially when you argue so much?" His response was, "If a quartet stays together for 35 years, the relationship cannot have been rancorous. There has to be a certain amount of mutual understanding, respect, and, yes, affection."]*

The Mandelring String Quartet

The Mandelring String Quartet makes a specialty of finding, performing, and recording works of unjustly forgotten or neglected composers. When the players discovered Berthold Goldschmidt, a composer whose age almost equaled that of the four young musicians' combined, they championed his music and became his close friends. In so doing they bridged the generation gap, helping to rejuvenate him and restore his creative powers. They discuss their relationship with Goldschmidt in this 1995 interview.

Champions of Unknown Music

The Mandelring Quartet of Neustadt, Germany, was formed in 1983 by the brothers Sebastian and Bernhard Schmidt, first violinist and cellist respectively, and their sister Nanette, second violinist; violist Nora Niggeling joined them in 1989. The group took its name from the street where the Schmidt siblings were born; literally meaning "almond crescent," it sounds like a piece of pastry. The Schmidts, however, explain that "Neustadt has an almost Italian climate; our area is full of almond trees and becomes a sea of pink blossoms in the spring." The family house is still home to their parents and host to the quartet's rehearsals.

The Mandelring won top prizes at the international string-quartet competitions in Munich and Evian in 1991, as well as the Paolo Borciani Competition at Reggio Emilia in 1994. By then, Niggeling had married and left the quartet; her place was taken by Michael Scheitzbach.

I first had a chance to chat with the players after hearing the dress rehearsal for their New York debut at the Frick Collection in November 1994. I was immediately impressed by their excellent intonation and balance, their expressive, homogeneous tone, and their truly fraternal spirit and rapport. I was also intrigued by their repertoire: in addition to performing the Classical and Romantic literature, they specialize in championing little-known composers, past and present, both in concert and on recordings. One of these is George Onslow (1784–1853), who, says Bernhard Schmidt, "was the son of an English earl and a rich man, but he had to settle in France after a family scandal. He could afford to compose for his own pleasure and wrote mostly chamber music, including 34 string quartets, 35 string quintets, sonatas, trios, sextets, a septet, even a nonet. Our father is a musicologist; he was at one time very interested in Onslow and has all his chamber music. Onslow remained relatively unknown, partly because neither the English nor the French would acknowledge him as their own or do anything to further his music. We are now trying to remedy this by playing through his collected works and trying to find and select the best—they do vary in quality. We have recorded three of the quartets, and more discs are being planned" [see discography on page 125].

The quartet's most recent recording pairs Brahms' Quartet No. 2 with a quartet by one of his contemporaries and friends, Felix Otto Dessoff (1835–92). "He was born in Leipzig," says Sebastian Schmidt, "and went to Vienna in 1860, where he conducted at the Opera and revived the then-dormant Philharmonic concerts. He also taught composition at the Conservatory and trained many excellent students. It was in Vienna that he met Brahms, whose works he had long admired and actively championed. He eventually left Vienna to direct various German orchestras and opera houses, but he continued to compose. He sent this string quartet to Brahms, asking for his opinion of it; Brahms found it 'friendly and amiable' and gratefully accepted Dessoff's dedication when it was published."

To me, the Mandelring's most interesting association is with Berthold Goldschmidt, a German composer who died in England a few years ago. Born in Hamburg in 1903, he emigrated to London in 1935, where I studied composition with him during the Second World War. When I met the Mandelring he was still living there, the only surviving member of an entire generation of promising German composers and other artists, such as Arnold Schoenberg, Erich Wolfgang Korngold, Kurt Weill, and Oscar Kokoschka, whose careers were destroyed by Hitler. "We met him in 1989 at a summer festival in Kiel where we were performing his Third Quartet," the players tell me, "and immediately became good friends. He had been rescued from 60 years of obscurity only a few years before through a lucky chance: someone had spotted the manuscript score of his early opera *The Magnificent Cuckold* in his apartment and staged it. A producer at London Decca saw the performance and decided to record the work."

I tell them that I have the recording and love it. "Yes—a lost masterpiece and, even better, its composer, were found again," Nanette Schmidt says. "Boosey & Hawkes are publishing his works, and they are being performed all over Europe. Germany has been producing

What they play

First violinist Sebastian Schmidt plays on an instrument made by Nicola Gagliano and uses a bow by the contemporary German maker Klaus Grünke. He uses a Corelli E string; the others are Dominants. Second violinist Nanette Schmidt uses the same string setup and plays a Gennaro Gagliano violin made in 1776. Her bow is by Morizot.

Current violist Roland Glassl plays an instrument made in 1998 by Johannes Glassl, his father. His bow was made by the contemporary French maker Stéphane Muller. Glassl uses Helicore strings with a Pirastro Permanent A. Cellist Bernhard Schmidt plays a François Aldric instrument made in Paris in 1808. His bow is a Sartory and he uses Pirastro Permanent strings.

Recordings

Brahms: Quartet in A Minor, Op. 51, No. 2; Dessoff: Quartet in F Major, Op. 7 (Lotus 03622).

Brahms: Piano Quintet in F Minor, Op. 34; Franck: Piano Quintet in F Minor (Hoepfner Classics).

Goldschmidt: Quartet No. 1 for Strings, Op. 8; Quartet for Clarinet and Strings. With Ib Hausman, clarinet (Largo 5117).

Goldschmidt: Quartets Nos. 2 and 3 for Strings (Largo 5115).

Mendelssohn: Quartet, Op. 12; Haydn: Quartet, Op. 77, No. 2 (German Broadcasting Corp.).

Onslow: Quartet in G Minor, Op. 9, No. 1; Quartet in F Minor, Op. 9, No. 3; Quartet in C Major, Op. 47 (CPO 999 060).

Onslow: Quartet in B-Flat Major, Op. 4, No. 1; Quartet in G Major, Op. 10, No. 1; Quartet in G Minor, Op. 46, No. 3 (CPO 999 329).

entire festivals of his music, and German record companies have been releasing both his early and his late works."

"What's so wonderful," I say, "is that he lived long enough to see himself rediscovered. When I knew him, he was a deeply discouraged man; he felt he was out of step with the compositional styles of the time. He used to say, 'What's the point of writing music if you cannot get it performed?' He was a shy, diffident person, so, though he was much respected in London's musical community, he was virtually unknown to the general public. He practically stopped composing for many years, scraping by on occasional calls as arranger or conductor and giving lessons—he was a wonderful, inspiring teacher. And then he started writing again in his 80s; that's perhaps the most remarkable thing about this whole story."

"Yes," says Bernhardt Schmidt, "he was revitalized by his sudden fame, and he never seemed to us like an old man. We love his quartets and have played all four of them, as well as the Clarinet Quintet, in public and on records."

For its Frick Gallery debut, the quartet programmed Goldschmidt's Second Quartet, written in 1936, a basically cheerful piece contrasting propulsive, dancing rhythms with lyrical, singing

Left to right, Bernhard Schmidt, Michael Scheitzbach, Nanette Schmidt, and Sebastian Schmidt.

melodies. The performance left no doubt of the players' affinity for the music and affection for the composer. Goldschmidt wrote his Fourth Quartet at the urging of Nanette Schmidt and dedicated it to the Mandelring Quartet with the words, "wholeheartedly acknowledging that my good friends amply deserve a composition all their own after their prolonged and intensive advocacy of my three previous quartets." Cast in one movement, it is a strong, powerfully expressive work.

I have a reunion with the Mandelring players when they are reinvited to the Frick Gallery in November 1999. They have a new violist, Roland Glassl, who won second prize at the 1994 William Primrose Memorial Competition in Guelph, Ontario. He is excellent, with a deep, warm, resonant tone, and already seems well-integrated into the group. The quartet's characteristically adventurous program includes György Ligeti's Quartet No. 2, which the players tell me they love for its changing colors, textures, and moods, and two movements of an unfinished quartet by the Viennese composer Alexander Zemlinsky (1871–1942), another of Hitler's victims who has only recently been rediscovered.

Clearly, the Mandelring's advocacy of both contemporary and unjustly neglected past composers is as ardent as ever, and its playing continues to grow in communicative ability and authority.

ABOUT THE AUTHOR

EDITH EISLER, *Strings* Magazine's corresponding editor from New York, is a violinist, violist, and teacher who has written for the publication since its inception in 1986. She began studying violin at the age of six in her native Vienna and later studied in Prague, with Max Rostal in London, and with Joseph Fuchs in New York. She performed solo and chamber music in Europe and North America and, for 11 years, ran Music among Friends, a series of house concerts performed by New York–based professionals. "Having been on the other side of the footlights most of my life gives me a certain perspective in interviewing players," she says. Besides profiling the string quartets in this book, she has written about many well-known soloists for *Strings,* including cellist Yo-Yo Ma and violinists Anne-Sophie Mutter and Midori, and covered numerous orchestras, teachers, seminars, and other musical events. She is, in addition, a contributor to *Stagebill, Chamber Music,* and the CD-reviews sections of Amazon.com and E-pulse.

OTHER TITLES FROM STRING LETTER PUBLISHING

Strings Magazine, 8 issues, $32.95

The leading periodical for string players and enthusiasts brings you global coverage of the string world through articles, interviews, reviews, transcriptions, profiles, letters, and lessons. With eight issues per year, *Strings* covers the personalities, music, news, events, instruments, and gear that matter. Each issue focuses on classical and new music while also exploring all musical genres in which string players are active.

For a free, no-risk copy of the latest issue, call (800) 827-6837 or visit www.stringsmagazine.com.

Musical Instrument Auction Price Guide, $44.95

Issued annually, illustrated with full-color plates of noteworthy instruments, the *Auction Price Guide* offers the most comprehensive information available on antique and handmade instrument and bow values. Asking and selling prices of instruments offered at the world's major auction houses are expressed in dollars, marks, pounds, and yen. A unique five-year summary by instrument and maker of high, low, and average prices shows market trends.

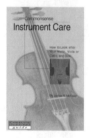

Commonsense Instrument Care Guide, 2nd edition, $9.95

Violin maker and dealer James N. McKean, past president of the American Federation of Violin and Bow Makers, has written the essential reference on maintaining the playability and value of violins, violas, and cellos and their bows.

ALSO IN THE *STRINGS* BACKSTAGE SERIES

21st-Century Violinists, Vol. 1, $12.95
21st-Century Violinists, Vol. 2, $12.95 (Fall 2000)

Two new collections of in-depth interviews with the world's preeminent string players offer students, teachers, and music lovers insights into the fascinating lives of classical violin soloists. Whether they're child prodigies just entering the stage or cultural icons whose careers have had a lasting influence on generations of players, these series of conversations reveal how they practice, how they work with other musicians, their performance secrets and anxieties, what moves and inspires them, and much more.

For more information on books from String Letter Publishing, or to place an order, please call Music Dispatch at (800) 637-2852 or (507) 454-2920, fax (507) 454-4042, or mail to Music Dispatch, PO Box 13920, Milwaukee, WI 53213. Visit String Letter Publishing on-line at www.stringletter.com.